PACIFIC COAST
FISH FINDER

A Guide to Marine Fish of the Pacific Coast of North America

RON RUSSO
illustrated by **ANN CAUDLE**

T0275186

Nature Study Guild Publishers
an imprint of Adventure**KEEN**

HOW TO USE THIS BOOK
If you have a fish you want to identify,
see pages 12–15.

If you want to know about the biology of:

- fish in general, pages 1–11
- sharks, p. 16
- salmon, p. 41
- rockfish, p. 53
- surfperch, p. 69
- tuna, p. 91
- flatfish, p. 96

If you've found a brittle or leathery-brown
case, see p. 19.

If you've found a tooth, see pages 20–21.

Key features
On some illustrations, lines point out traits
important to identification.

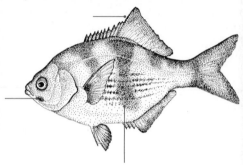

This book includes some of the common marine fish you're likely to encounter while
fishing or diving along the Pacific Coast. Many other species are known to occur here.

Ron Russo was the chief naturalist for the East Bay Regional Park District in Oakland, California.
He received the 1989 Fellow Award of the National Association for Interpretation and the 2017
Thomas Say Award for contributions to science and education.

Ann Caudle teaches Science Illustration at California State University, Monterey Bay.

© 2024 Ron Russo (text), Ann Caudle (illustrations); © 1990 Nature Study Guild • ISBN 978-0-912550-40-4 •
Printed in China • Cataloging-in-Publication data is available from the Library of Congress • naturestudy.com

FISH BIOLOGY

In the course of evolution, fish have exploited nearly every aquatic habitat. From freezing Arctic waters to the hot pools of Death Valley, fish have adapted to diverse conditions. Today, over 32,000 species inhabit the seas, lakes, rivers, ponds, and the tiniest of streams on Earth. Worldwide, fish populations are being seriously threatened by overfishing, illegal fishing, pollution, habitat destruction, and other environmental changes.

COMMON FEATURES

There are three main groups of fish: **jawless fish** (hagfish, lampreys); **cartilaginous fish** (sharks, rays, chimaeras); and **bony fish** (salmon, perch). The fish in each group vary in size, shape, color, and ecological roles. But all fish tend to share some common features that aid in their survival.

SKIN, SCALES, AND SLIME

Skin is an important organ. It protects and encloses a fish's body and regulates oxygen exchange, excretion, and water pressure. It has sense organs, nerves, and blood vessels, as well as pigment-bearing cells called chromatophores. The skin is protected by slime, secreted by its mucous-producing cells and, in many species, by hard overlapping scales.

You can often tell a fish's age by counting the microscopic growth rings in its scales. Evidence of disease, injury, starvation, pollution, and other unfavorable conditions in a fish's life can also be found as a microscopic record in fish scales.

FINS

Fins are supported by soft cartilage or by hard, bony spines or rays. They're used as propellers, rudders, stabilizers, brakes, and hydroplanes, or as ingenious anti-roll devices to maintain proper orientation. Some fish use their fins as limbs to "walk" along the bottom. Rockfishes and surfperches often use fins to signal aggression or interest in mating. Some sharks use pectoral fins and arching their back to warn of imminent attack.

VISION

In most bony fish, the position of the eyes allows a field of view extending nearly 360 degrees, letting them see prey and predators. Most fish are considered farsighted. Fish living in dark, deep, or murky waters tend to have larger eyes than ones in light, shallow, or clear waters. Many bony fish detect color.

HEARING AND SOUND

Fish have three structures sensitive to sound. High-frequency sound is picked up by the inner ear and by the swim bladder. Low frequencies are detected by the lateral-line system, a well-defined canal that runs along the midbody and branches over the head and face. Within these canals are sensitive hair cells that are bent by low-frequency vibrations.

Some species make sound by grinding teeth in the back of the mouth; moving two bones in the pectoral girdle; or by vibrating the walls of the swim bladder with special muscles. Such sounds function in courtship, spawning, defense, and migration. Sounds enable schooling fish to warn each other of danger.

BREATHING

Oxygen is absorbed and carbon dioxide is released as water passes over the intricate network of capillaries in a fish's gills. Fish have a coughing or sneezing reflex to eject foreign matter that might otherwise clog the gills and cause suffocation. Some fish can absorb atmospheric oxygen by gulping air at the surface.

COLOR

Pigments are housed in specialized skin cells called chromatophores. Each chromatophore has a specific color. Nerves connected to chromatophores control intensity of color by concentrating or dispersing the pigment. In this way, fish can change color to match their surroundings, to defend territory, or to advertise readiness for mating.

The intensity of some color is influenced by secretions from the pituitary gland. Other apparent color is produced not by pigment, but by refraction of light reflected back to the viewer. Iridescent greens, blues, and browns are produced this way: Silver color is due to the reflection of light off of crystalline guanine, a metabolic waste product. Black pigments are also waste products.

Many fish have dark backs and light bellies. This pattern, called counter shading, compensates for the sunlight on the back and the shadow on the belly, so that the fish are less noticeable when viewed from the side. Counter-shaded fish blend with the lighter background of the surface when viewed from below and with the dark background of the bottom when viewed from above.

SWIM BLADDER

There is a gas-filled swim bladder between the stomach and the spine of most bony fish. It controls buoyancy. As a fish rises, dissolved gas leaves the blood and expands the bladder, increasing buoyancy. When the fish sinks, increased pressure forces bladder gas back into the blood, decreasing buoyancy. The buoyancy stabilizes as the fish holds to a given depth. Bony fish without swim bladders (flatfish and sculpins) habitually rest on the bottom. Nonbony sharks and rays also lack swim bladders.

SALT BALANCE

All fish have dissolved salts essential to survival in their flesh and blood. These salts are maintained at specific levels of concentration. The levels often differ from the concentrations in the surrounding water. Water tends to move from an area of low salt concentration to an area of higher concentration. It can either leave or enter the fish's body through the membranes covering its gills, mouth, and pharynx. This process can alter the salt concentrations, making the fish either too salty or not salty enough. Fish have adapted to this problem in several ways. The bodies of freshwater fish have higher salt concentrations than the surrounding water. They are, then, in danger of flooding their cells. To compensate, they produce high volumes of urine.

In marine bony fish, the reverse is true. They are less salty than sea water and in constant danger of dehydration. To compensate, marine fish drink 10–40% of their body weight daily, excreting excess salts through special cells in their gills and producing very little urine.

Sharks and rays, on the other hand, have slightly higher salt concentrations than the sea. They prevent dilution of the required salt level by keeping high levels of urea in their blood, which equalizes the internal and external environments.

When marine fish enter freshwater, they slowly reverse their normal habits to maintain the proper balance of salts.

SCHOOLING

Anchovies, herring, mackerel, smelts, tuna, some rockfish, and other species often form groups, or schools, of up to thousands of like-size fish. Simple aggregations of fish disperse when startled, but schools draw together, tightening up their formation when startled.

To some predators, a school may appear as a single giant organism. Fish attacking a school may also be confused and deterred by the difficulty of focusing on any given individual within the school, as its members dart and turn in near-perfect unison. The many sets of eyes in a school help schooling fish to detect and warn each other of danger and make foraging more efficient. But it's no guarantee of survival. Barracuda, tuna, thresher sharks, and some other predators are adept at feeding on schooling fish. Finally, schooling makes it easier to find a mate and successfully spawn.

PARASITES

No fish is totally free of parasites. Various small crustaceans called copepods penetrate the protective slime to feed between the scales of fish on their body juices. The bodies and fin edges of sharks often bear such external parasites. A marine leech, *Branchellion lobata,* regularly attaches itself to the lining of the mouth, the claspers, the surface of the eyes, and the soft tissues at the free edges of fins in a variety of sharks. The gill louse, *Elthusa vulgaris,* attaches itself to the gills of both bony and cartilaginous fish. It feeds on the hormones and nutrients in the blood. Fish are not totally at the mercy of external parasites, including copepods and worms. They routinely scrape against rocks or sand to dislodge their hitchhikers. Some fish use the cleaning services of other fish or shrimp that specialize in removing parasites.

Internal parasites—tapeworms, roundworms, threadworms, and flatworms—are common in intestines, hearts, livers, muscles, and blood. Normally, these do not imperil the life of the host fish. **CAUTION: Be sure to cook fish thoroughly before consumption.**

LOCATIONS IN TEXT

Locations in parentheses indicate instances where the behavior of a species at the given locality is reported in scientific literature. The behavior in question takes place elsewhere within the range of the species, but we cite only the location where it has been reliably observed.

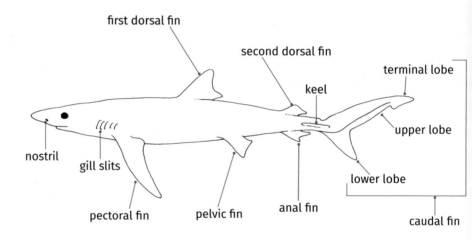

(Fish illustrated is a blue shark.)

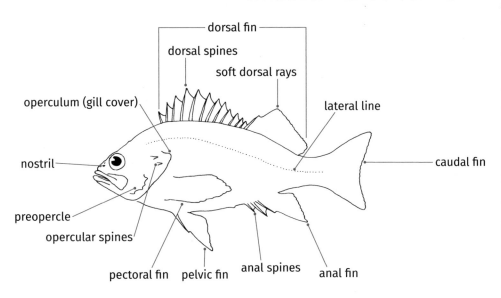

(Fish illustrated is a rockfish.)

surfperch

blue rockfish

kelpfish

senorita

kelp rockfish

Garibaldi

vermillion rockfish

greenling

wolf eel

leopard shark

spotted sand bass

electric ray

lingcod

cabezon

flounder

VERTICAL DISTRIBUTION OF INSHORE FISH
(shallow water)

This illustration shows some fish in their typical vertical location in inshore areas. Rough seas usually force fish toward the bottom for protection, while calm water encourages dispersal and movement to higher levels for some species like the blue rockfish.

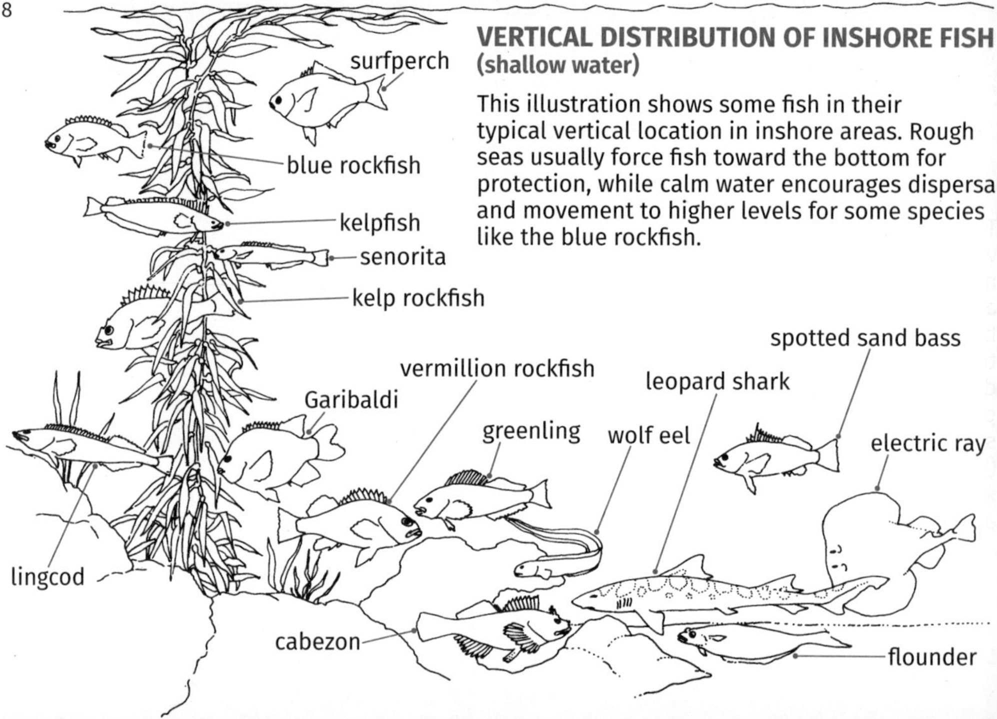

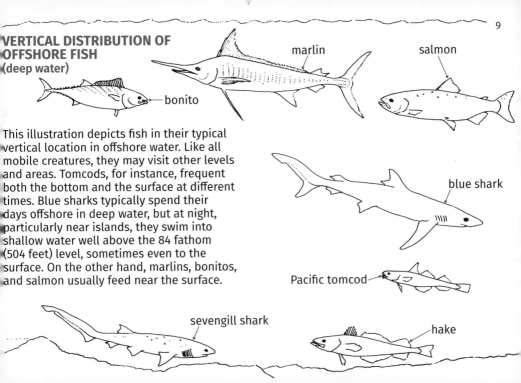

VERTICAL DISTRIBUTION OF OFFSHORE FISH
(deep water)

bonito

marlin

salmon

This illustration depicts fish in their typical vertical location in offshore water. Like all mobile creatures, they may visit other levels and areas. Tomcods, for instance, frequent both the bottom and the surface at different times. Blue sharks typically spend their days offshore in deep water, but at night, particularly near islands, they swim into shallow water well above the 84 fathom (504 feet) level, sometimes even to the surface. On the other hand, marlins, bonitos, and salmon usually feed near the surface.

blue shark

Pacific tomcod

sevengill shark

hake

Arrows show which way the food goes.

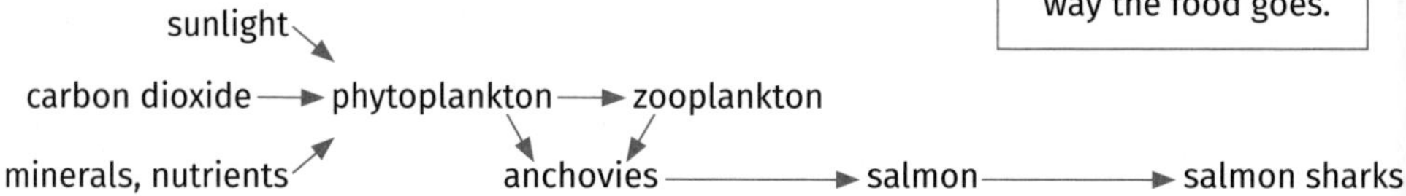

sunlight

carbon dioxide ⟶ phytoplankton ⟶ zooplankton

minerals, nutrients ⟶ anchovies ⟶ salmon ⟶ salmon sharks

Pacific Coast waters have upwelling currents, which bring up a mix of minerals and organic compounds representing the remains of countless creatures that die and settle in deep water. The food chain illustrated above begins when phytoplankton, minute drifting plants, use these minerals and nutrients, plus carbon dioxide and the energy in sunlight, to produce oxygen and their own food. The plants multiply and become food for the zooplankton: tiny drifting animals like copepods, and the larvae of crabs, shrimp, barnacles, etc. Plankton are strained from the water by anchovies, which in turn are eaten by salmon, which are eaten by salmon sharks.

In the above food chain, each link represents a transfer of energy, from prey to predator. The predator burns up some of this energy for its own metabolism, then uses the rest to grow larger and, if lucky, to reproduce.

Energy accumulates in the larger fish as they eat the smaller ones. An anchovy consumes countless minute planktonic creatures in its life. In turn, it takes hundreds of anchovies to produce a 20-pound salmon, and many salmon to produce a full-grown salmon shark. The salmon shark is the top predator in its food chain, just as white sharks, sperm whales, and humans are in theirs.

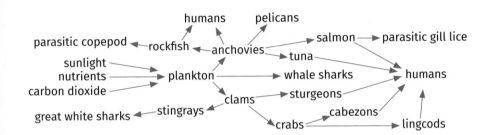

The above food web outlines a few of the interactions among marine organisms. Every element in the web depends directly or indirectly on phytoplankton. These relationships become vastly more complex than a simple food chain.

A complete food web would include all relationships between species: the predators and parasites; the many ways species use each other for shelter, transportation, and protection; the production and recycling of carbon dioxide, oxygen, and metabolic wastes; the settling and recycling of organic material from ocean depths . . . and more. Many of these relationships have been identified, but most remain to be discovered.

However, biologists do know enough to understand that reckless tampering with this complex web, whether through reduction or extermination of species or by pollution of their environment, endangers all life, including our own.

Fish on the next four pages are arranged by shape (but they are not drawn precisely to scale). See page indicated for more detail.

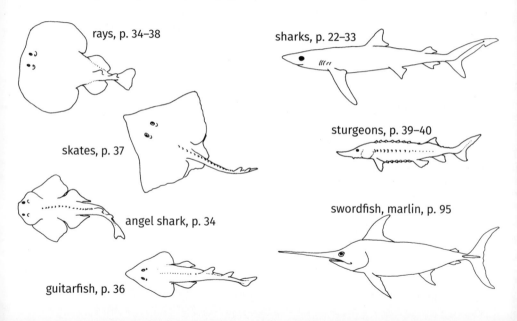

rays, p. 34–38

sharks, p. 22–33

skates, p. 37

sturgeons, p. 39–40

angel shark, p. 34

swordfish, marlin, p. 95

guitarfish, p. 36

sheepshead, p. 88

opaleye, p. 90

Garibaldi, p. 85

surfperches, p. 69–78

flatfish, flounder, p. 104

blacksmith, p. 86

14

yellowtail,
jack mackerel,
p. 84

cabezon,
red Irish lord,
p. 49

Pacific mackerel,
skipjack, p. 92

corbina, p. 83

bonito,
albacore, p. 93
tuna, p. 94

croaker, p. 83

greenlings, p. 51

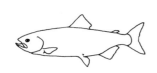

salmon, p. 43
steelhead, p. 42

sculpins, p. 50

striped bass, p. 79

lingcod, p. 52

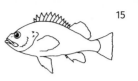

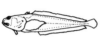 sand bass, kelp bass, p. 81	rockfish, p. 53-68
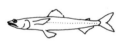 midshipman, p. 45	senorita, p. 88 
 lizardfish, p. 45	barracuda, p. 87 
 cod, p. 46 tomcod, p. 47	wolf-eel, p. 87
 smelt, eulachon, p. 44 grunion, p. 47	monkeyface eel, p. 89 
hake, p. 46	kelpfish, p. 89 

SHARK BIOLOGY

Few other creatures in the sea elicit the intense, bone-chilling response in people who swim, dive, or sail that sharks do. But of more than 500 known shark species, only about a dozen attack people, and they usually do so only in response to provocation, or perhaps because they sense distress in the victim, or they mistake a human for a sea lion. Most sharks are either too small to bother people; they live in deep water; or they're harmless giants who feed on plankton, fish, or other small creatures. They range in size from a 6-inch Japanese species to the 38-foot whale shark. They occupy all the oceans. A few species swim well up into rivers, and one lives in Lake Nicaragua, in Central America.

Unfortunately, the biology of most shark species is not well-known because few specimens have ever been examined and observed. Our understanding is based on some species that have been studied thoroughly.

Sharks have a cartilaginous skeleton instead of bones. Their razor-sharp teeth, made of dentine, are a modified form of the scales covering their skin. Sharks lack swim bladders, so they must constantly swim or rest on the bottom. They also lack single, external gill covers. Instead, each set of gills is exposed directly to the outside through thin slits in the sides of their head.

Just under the skin of the face and head, sharks have a network of jelly-filled canals or tubes that connect to the lateral line, then open to the outside through pores. These canals, called the Ampullae of Lorenzini, enable the shark to detect weak electrical fields at short range, and thereby find prey in total darkness or buried in sand. Just behind the eyes of most sharks are tiny holes called **spiracles,** which are vestigial gill slits that provide oxygenated blood directly to the eyes and brain through a separate blood vessel. The position of the mouth on the underside and back from the snout allows sharks to sample or taste and smell items before biting them. Teeth are arranged in rows along the edges of each jaw, with several replacements lined up behind each tooth. A damaged or lost tooth is replaced in a matter of days, with no loss of feeding efficiency to the bearer.

Although the physical features of skates and rays are quite different, the biology is generally similar to that of sharks.

SHARK REPRODUCTION

The evolutionary success of sharks is partly due to their reproductive adaptations. They have three basic reproductive modes. Each begins with internal fertilization. Males have specialized pelvic fins shaped like stout tubes that guide sperm directly into females.

Some species, including all skates, are **oviparous,** producing eggs that develop outside the parent, enclosed in leathery cases.

Most sharks are **ovoviviparous,** hatching the eggs inside the uterine canals of the female. The embryos are nourished either from large egg yolks or by ingesting the yolks of their litter mates. Although such females produce relatively few young, the pups spend their most vulnerable period inside their parent. After completing their development, they are born relatively large, as near-perfect replicas of their parents.

The most advanced reproductive mode is in those sharks that are **viviparous,** having embryos initially dependent on yolk but later nourished directly by the parent through a placental connection.

Because of their relatively low reproductive rate, sharks are particularly vulnerable to human ignorance, overfishing, finning, and poor fishery management. Exaggerated movies of the 1970s unleashed a misinformed, overzealous, and maniacal shark-hunting craze in North America that lasted too long. The depletion of some species is of critical concern to researchers seeking, for instance, to study sharks' resistance to heart disease and cancer. But we have a greater interest in the survival of sharks. They are important predators and scavengers, and they no doubt play other roles in the ocean we know little about.

SHARK CONSERVATION

Over the last several decades, shark populations worldwide have plummeted largely due to the use of longlines and gillnets in commercial fishing. The continued practice of shark finning has resulted in the loss of millions of sharks worldwide. Some scientists estimate that over 100 million sharks are killed each year due to commercial efforts. Additionally, a naturally occurring ciliated protozoa, called *Miamiensis avidus,* infects the brain and nasal tissues of mostly leopard sharks in San Francisco Bay, California, causing disorientation, stranding, and death in thousands of sharks. High runoff of contaminated water is thought to be associated with these annual mortalities.

Along the Pacific Coast, there is only one elasmobranch, the great white shark, that has any kind of protection. Anglers cannot attempt to catch or keep any great white sharks. Other species, including the leopard soupfin, blunt-nosed sixgill, and sevengill sharks, are locally targeted for their meat. Because sharks are apex predators and play a key role in the ecosystem of all marine waters, fishing restrictions, especially in and around nursery areas, should be imposed.

ELASMOBRANCH STRANDINGS

For more than 70 years, sharks and rays within San Francisco Bay have been found seasonally stranded on beaches at low tide. Leopard sharks and bat rays were most common, but other elasmobranchs have been affected. In 2017, scientists were finally able to determine the cause of these strandings, which appears to be a meningoencephalitis infection (inflammation of the brain and protective membranes) induced by the ciliated protozoan pathogen *Miamiensis avidus.* This condition may also affect salmon sharks, great white sharks, brown smoothhound sharks, Pacific angel sharks, and other species of elasmobranchs along the Pacific Coast.

| horn shark | swell shark | starry skate | California skate | big skate |
| 125mm (avg.) | 90–125mm | 71–78mm | 70–85mm | 265–305mm |

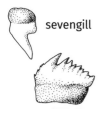
sevengill

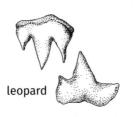
leopard

gray smoothhound

brown smoothhound

soupfin

dogfish

swell

horn

(Teeth are not drawn to scale.)

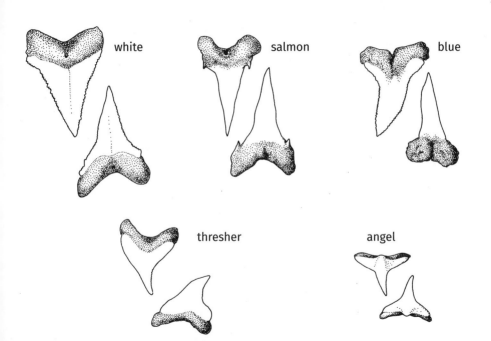

21

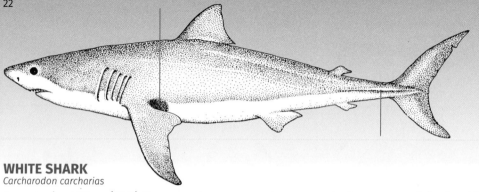

WHITE SHARK
Carcharodon carcharias

Average size 460 cm (15 ft). Some reach 640 cm (21 ft) and 4,800 lbs or larger. Color varies from lead white to slate brown or blue above to dirty white below. Key features are torpedo-shaped snout, triangular teeth with serrated edges, and black area at base of pectoral fins. A strong swimmer, it hunts in shallow water. Specimens under 3 m (9 ft) eat various fish, including rockfish, tuna, bat rays, and other sharks. Larger white sharks eat mostly marine mammals. Once an attack begins, it's swift, determined, and often fatal. Known to attack surfers, bathers, divers, even boats. Ovoviviparous. Newborn young are about 129 cm (51 in). Found worldwide. On Pacific Coast, Alaska to southern California, but most abundant between Tomales Bay and Monterey, where large colonies of its primary prey, seals and sea lions, occur. Gulf of California is thought to be one of many nursery grounds.

BLUE SHARK
Prionace glauca

Average size 240 cm (8 ft), with larger specimens to 380 cm (12 ft). Dark indigo-blue on top, bright blue laterally. Key features are blue color, long nose, pectoral fins, and large eyes. Eats small schooling fish like anchovies, sardines, and herring. Will eat captured salmon, rockfish, squid, and wounded marine mammals. Viviparous. After gestation of 9–12 months, female usually bears 25–50 pups, each about 40–51 cm (16–20 in) long.

Births of up to 135 pups are known. Young blue sharks, 76 cm (30 in) long, have been seen cruising at surface near Farallon Islands in August. Adults are pelagic, around islands, particularly at night. Rare near mainland. Blue shark lives in deep, clear-blue water. Ranges widely along entire Pacific Coast. Generally sluggish, with impressive bursts of speed and feeding frenzies. A "potentially" dangerous shark.

THRESHER SHARK
Alopias vulpinus

Individuals 300–500 cm (10–16 ft) are common. Some reach 610 cm (20 ft) and 1,000 lbs. Color varies from dark metallic brown to near black on top, with a white underside. Arching tail, used to stun prey, is distinctive. Eats mainly schooling fish like shad, mackerel, and sardines, but also squid. Charges into a school, then returns to swallow wounded fish. Ovoviviparous, four to six pups born per litter, 137–155 cm (54–61 in) each. Females are sexually mature at 10 feet. This is a pelagic, deep-water shark, mostly caught on longline below 100 fathoms. Some caught near surface. Along coast from British Columbia to California.

SALMON SHARK
Lamna ditropis

Length to 300 cm (10 ft). Dark bluish-gray to bluish-black above, with an abrupt change to white on the belly. This fast-swimming pelagic species migrates along the coast in groups of 30–40 individuals, following schools of salmon. Eats salmon, tomcods, and mackerel in the north and squid, lanternfish, and sauries in the south.

The salmon shark is a major predator of salmon and destroys salmon-fishing gear. Ovoviviparous, two to four pups born per litter, 65–70 cm (26–28 in) long. From Bering Sea to San Diego.

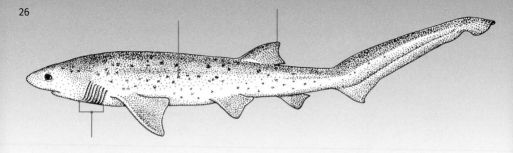

SEVENGILL SHARK
Notorhynchus cepedianus

Average size of commonly caught specimens 70–125 cm (28–49 in). Largest recorded is 296 cm (9 ft), but larger specimens 300–400 cm probably exist. Gray to reddish-brown with irregular black spots (distinct for each individual) over the sides and back; white belly. Albinism is known in this shark. Key features are broad head, large mouth, seven gill slits (instead of five), a single dorsal fin, and black spots. Eats chimaeras, mackerel, and other small sharks. Feeds on longline-caught sharks in bays, leaving only heads. Ovoviviparous. Litter size of 80 pups or more. Young about 50 cm (20 in) at birth. Adult females apparently enter bays and shallow eelgrass areas to give birth. Immatures common in Tomales, San Francisco, and Monterey Bays. Species ranges throughout Pacific and Indian Oceans. Known to attack divers. Swims constantly; seldom rests on bottom. Has been called "Lord of the Depths." A potentially dangerous species.

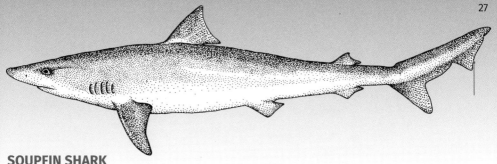

SOUPFIN SHARK
Galeorhinus galeus

Average size 165 cm (65 in) for males, 175 cm (69 in) for females; maximum size to 200 cm (79 in). Dark bluish-gray to dark gray above; white below. Has sharp teeth. An opportunistic feeder, eating sardines, flounder, rockfish, mackerel, and squid. Ovoviviparous. Gestation of about 12 months; newborn pups are 35 cm (14 in). Some born in Tomales and San Francisco Bays, but major pupping grounds appear to be south of Point Conception. Males are mature at about 155 cm (61 in), females at 170 cm (67 in). There is some segregation by sex, with males abundant off northern California and females abundant off southern California. Range is British Columbia to Baja California to Chile and Peru. Historically, this shark was an important commercial source of vitamin A, fillets, and fins for soup. Overfishing in nursery areas and finning have depleted the populations.

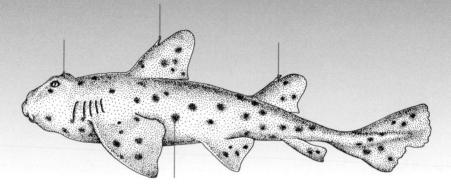

HORN SHARK
Heterodontus francisci

Normal adult size about 90 cm (35 in), with some to 122 cm (48 in). Light to dark brown above, light beige on belly, with small black spots over entire body. Has sharp spine in front of each dorsal fin. Characteristic ridge over eye protects eye while shark nudges rocks in pursuit of food. Eats crabs, shrimp, clam necks, and small fish. Oviparous. Lays screw-shaped, chitinous egg cases; embryos develop and hatch in 6–9 months at 15–17 cm (6–7 in). A sluggish, bottom-dwelling, nocturnal shark. Found in shallow-to-deep water, central California to Gulf of California.

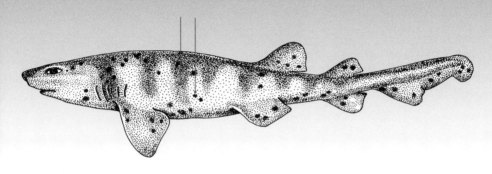

SWELL SHARK
Cephaloscyllium ventriosum

Normal adult size 90–110 cm (35–43 in). Brown areas and dark-brown spots across back. Eats small fish, crabs, shrimp, and worms. Oviparous. Lays chitinous eggs, which hatch 7.5–10 months later. Pups measure 14–15 cm (6 in). Common in 5–20 fathoms, but strays to 160 fathoms. Prefers rocky, algae-covered areas. A sluggish bottom dweller. When disturbed, this shark can double its girth by swallowing water or air as a defense. Common from Monterey south.

GRAY SMOOTHHOUND SHARK
Mustelus californicus

Adults are about 116 cm (46 in). Brown to dark gray above, white below. Spiracle behind eye. Albinism occurs in this species. Eats primarily crabs. Feeds inshore, in shallow bays, sounds, and rocky shores. Viviparous. Gestation 9–12 months. Litters of 3–16 pups, measuring 20–30 cm (8–12 in), born in spring. Found down to 25 fathoms, but usually in 3 fathoms or less. Rare in northern California, more common in southern California and Mexico. Common in inshore waters of central California in winter.

BROWN SMOOTHHOUND, SAND SHARK

Mustelus henlei

Adults are 65–97 cm (26–38 in). Bronze, reddish-brown above, white below. Has small teeth. Eats shrimp, worms, crabs, small fish, and fish eggs. In turn, it is eaten by sea lions and sevengill sharks. Pups known to be eaten by large rockfish and other sharks. Viviparous. Litter of 6–12 pups, measuring about 21 cm (8 in), born in open bays and eelgrass beds in spring. Brown smoothhounds travel in schools. Range is from Oregon to Peru, but it's most common in bays north of Monterey.

LEOPARD SHARK
Triakis semifasciata

Average size 150 cm (59 in) for males, 180 cm (71 in) for females. Maximum 210 cm (83 in). Large sizes now rare in San Francisco Bay, due to overfishing. This popular sport species is easily recognized by its whitish-to-light-gray body with large black bars and dots, which increase in number with age. Albinism occurs. Often bury their face into sand and mud in pursuit of echiuroid worms, ghost shrimp, blue mud shrimp, and clam siphons. Also eats small fish, fish eggs, octopi, crabs, and tunicates. Often feeds intertidally. In bays, travels in size- and sometimes sex-segregated schools. Often rests on bottom. Females are mature at about 110 cm (43 in). Ovoviviparous. Gestation 9–12 months. Litter size to 34 pups, measuring 18–20 cm (7–8 in), born March–May, in or near marsh channels and eelgrass beds of Humboldt, Tomales, and San Francisco Bays; Elkhorn Slough; and similar sites south. Pups nearly double their size in first year. Pups are vulnerable to shallow-water shrimp harvesting and aquarists. Adults and juveniles vulnerable to seasonal outbreaks of a ciliated protozoan, *Miamiensis avidus,* responsible for dead sharks washing up on Bay Area beaches. A timid, harmless, inshore shark that ranges from Oregon to Gulf of California.

SPINY DOGFISH SHARK
Squalus suckleyi

Adults 75–130 cm (30–51 in). Slate gray to brownish-gray with small white spots and deep-green eyes. Sharp spine in front of each dorsal fin. Albinism known. An opportunistic feeder that eats fish, fish eggs, shrimp, crabs, and octopi. Males mature at 80–100 cm (31–39 in) or 11 years of age. Females mature at 100–124 cm (39–49 in) or 18–20 years of age. Ovoviviparous. Gestation of 22–24 months (one of the longest next to that of elephants). Pups are 20–30 cm (8–12 in) long, 2–11 per litter. Before birth, they turn inside mother to emerge head-first, avoiding spine damage to her vent. Spiny dogfish travels in schools of hundreds, sometimes thousands. Damages commercial fishing nets and bait. Its liver oil was once an important source of vitamin A. Found to 400 fathoms or more. In North Pacific from Bering Sea to Baja California.

PACIFIC ANGEL SHARK *Squatina californica*
Average size 100 cm (39 in). May reach 155 cm
(61 in). Sandy gray to reddish-brown with dark
spots. Characterized by flat body, wide toothy
mouth, and expanded pectoral fins. Eats fish.
Ovoviviparous. Reproductive biology not well
known. Nocturnal. By day, found buried in
sand, mud, or near rocks or ledges. Anyone
handling this shark must be wary of bite.
From southern Alaska to Baja California.

PACIFIC ELECTRIC RAY *Torpedo californica*
Length 91–137 cm (36–54 in). Bluish-gray to
brownish-gray with many dark spots. Head
not distinguishable. Eats crabs, shrimp,
worms, other invertebrates, and fish.
Ovoviviparous. Powerful electric current can
stun prey and human handlers. Parasitic
Cooper's nutmeg snail anesthetizes local area
of resting ray, to penetrate and feed on ray's
body fluids without being shocked. Found
buried in sand or mud, down to 150 fathoms.
From British Columbia to Baja California.
Found buried in sand, mud, down to 150
fathoms. British Columbia to Baja California.

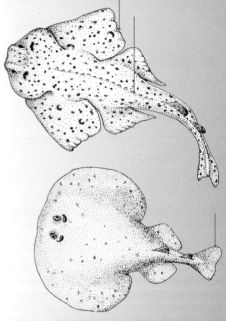

CAUTION: DO NOT HANDLE.

THORNBACK RAY
Platyrhinoidis triseriata

Length to 91 cm (36 in). Brown, grayish-brown, or olive-brown over back. Key features are two large dorsal fins and three rows of large, hooked spines on back and tail. Eats sand-dwelling crabs, shrimp, worms, and clams. Buries itself in fine sand and mud. Found down to 25 fathoms. From Monterey to Baja California. Rare north of Monterey.

BAT RAY
Myliobatis californica

To 182 cm (72 in) wide. Dark brown, olive, or blackish-brown. Key features are raised, massive head and single spine at base of whiplike tail. Slimy, no scales. Mouth has platelike teeth used in crushing clams. Bat ray also eats echiuroid worms, shrimp, crabs, oysters, bay mussels, and snails. Exposes clams by flapping wings, displacing mud and leaving large pot holes behind in the process. Ovoviviparous. Gestation about 12 months. Ten or fewer young, about 22 cm (9 in) wide, born in summer. Often in large schools. From Oregon to Gulf of California.

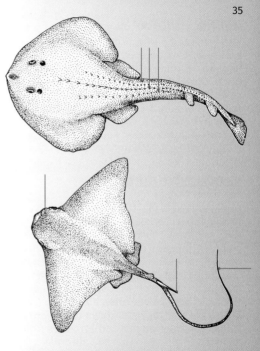

ROUND STINGRAY *Urolophus halleri*

To 56 cm (22 in) long. Brownish or grayish-brown with yellow spots or reticulations. Uses large spine, midway on tail, in defense against predators such as sharks. Eats clams, shrimp, crabs, and small fish. Ovoviviparous. Large numbers of adults congregate off beaches to mate and give birth. One to six young born inshore in late summer. Found on sandy, muddy bottoms, also in bays and sloughs to 12 fathoms. Ranges from Eureka to Panama.

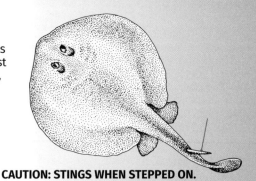

SHOVELNOSE GUITARFISH
Rhinobatos productus

Females 168 cm (5.5 ft), males smaller. Sandy brown above. Long, pointed snout and single row of spines on back are characteristic. Eats crabs, shrimp, worms, clams, and small fish. Ovoviviparous. Up to 28 young per litter, born measuring about 15 cm (6 in) long. Often on bottom; covers itself with sand and mud. Nomadic, gregarious, often abundant. Lives in shallow coastal water down to 8.5 fathoms. Found in bays, sloughs, and estuaries from San Francisco Bay to Gulf of California.

CAUTION: STINGS WHEN STEPPED ON.

BIG SKATE
Raja binoculata

To 183 cm (6 ft), some to 244 cm (8 ft).
Gray, brown, reddish-brown, or blackish,
with concentric zones of white spots around
dark eyespot on each wing. Eats crabs,
shrimp, and bottom fish. Oviparous. Eggs
up to 30 cm long with several embryos per
egg case.

Common at moderate depths to 60 fathoms,
from Bering Sea to Point Conception; rare
south to Baja California.

CALIFORNIA SKATE
Raja inornata

To 76 cm (30 in). Olive-brown, sometimes
with dark mottling and dark eyespots.
Eats crabs, shrimp, clams, and bottom
fish. Oviparous. Eggs have long horns, one
embryo per egg case. Common inshore and
in bays. Occasionally found in deep water,
to 366 fathoms, from Straits of Juan de
Fuca to Baja California.

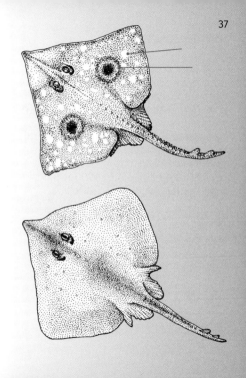

STARRY SKATE
Raja stellulata

To 76 cm (30 in). Brown, gray-brown, often with light spots; has two eyespots with yellow centers and brown rings. This is our spiniest skate; much of its upper surface is covered with prickles. Eats crabs, shrimp, clams, and fish. Oviparous. Eggs have lines; one embryo per egg case. In north, born June–July. Found on sand-mud bottom to 400 fathoms, from Bering Sea to Baja California.

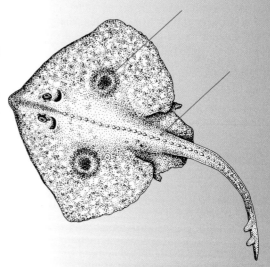

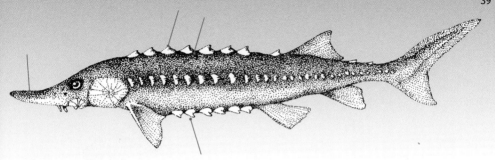

GREEN STURGEON
Acipenser medirostris

To 213 cm (84 in). Grayish-white to olive-green. Key features are bony plates on back and along sides, concave snout, and long barbels. Has a skeleton that is mostly cartilage, like that of sharks, but sturgeons are primitive bony fish. Eats clams, shrimp, crabs, and worms in bays and estuaries by slurping them out of mud with protrusile mouth. Moves into freshwater to spawn, where it eats crayfish, snails, and insect larvae. Taste buds are outside of mouth. Large females lay 2–5 million eggs, which hatch in two weeks to three months. From Bering Sea to Ensenada.

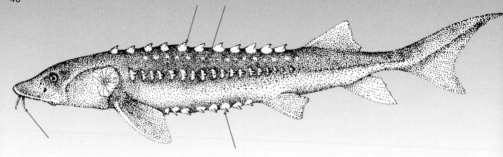

WHITE STURGEON
Acipenser transmontanus

To 609 cm (240 in). May exceed 1,500 lbs–largest North American freshwater fish. Gray, light below. Has more bony plates along sides, and barbels closer to snout tip, than green sturgeon. Spends most, if not all, of its time in freshwater. Moves upstream in winter or spring, downstream in summer. Eats snails, clams, crayfish, spawned-out eulachon. Lays millions of eggs, in spring or summer. Young eat amphipods, mysid shrimp. Matures after 11 years. From Gulf of Alaska to Ensenada.

SALMON BIOLOGY

Salmon and steelhead trout migrate from salt to freshwater to spawn. Such fish are called **anadromous.** The young leave freshwater to spend from one to four years in the ocean, some migrating thousands of miles out to sea. When mature, they use stars, moon, currents, electric and magnetic fields, and their sense of smell as navigational aids in relocating the mouth of their home stream, which they enter to spawn.

Once in freshwater, the sense of smell becomes their primary guide in their journey upstream to shallow spawning areas. Males undergo tremendous physical changes in color and shape prior to spawning.

After they reach the spawning area, females excavate gravel nests with their tails, displacing pebbles and silt. Males quickly fertilize the eggs, while females move upstream a meter or so to excavate another nest. The displaced gravel often washes downstream to bury the previously laid eggs. To hatch successfully, the eggs must be surrounded by pebbles and oxygenated water. Silt destroys eggs and newly hatched fish.

Young salmon and steelhead quickly become imprinted with the specific odor of their home stream. This will guide them back to the same stream as adults. Mortality is high from egg to adult. Dams, diversions, erosion, and silt are major problems that have reduced or eliminated salmon and steelhead in many rivers and streams.

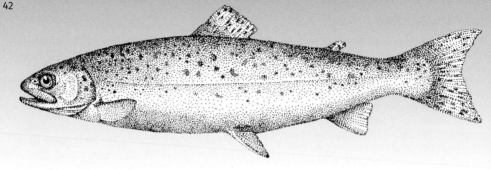

STEELHEAD TROUT
Oncorhynchus mykiss

To 114 cm (45 in) and 40 lbs. In the sea, bluish above, silver below, with black spots on back and fins. Often a pink-to-red stripe on side. Mouth white. Greenish and less silver in freshwater. A steelhead is a rainbow trout that migrates to sea. Eats various crustaceans and fish. Adult spawns in stream gravel fall and winter. Young live in freshwater up to four years, then at sea for two to three years. Adults survive spawning. From Bering Sea to San Luis Obispo County.

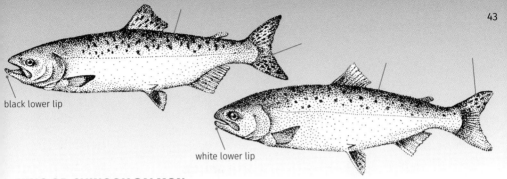

black lower lip

white lower lip

43

KING OR CHINOOK SALMON
Oncorhynchus tshawytscha

To 147 cm (58 in). Normally under 50 lbs but some to 100 lbs. Greenish-blue to gray or black above with irregular black spots. Gums black at base of teeth. Eats various crustaceans and fish. Spawning runs occur in fall and spring. Most young go to sea soon after hatching, but some may remain in stream. May range 1,000 miles out into Pacific. Most return to stream of birth in four or five years; others return later. From Bering Sea to San Diego.

SILVER OR COHO SALMON
Oncorhynchus kisutch

To 98 cm (38 in), 31 lbs. Metallic blue back with black spots, silvery below. Gums white at base of teeth. Eats various organisms, including fish, squid, and crustaceans. Spawns in fall, early winter, then dies. Young stay in freshwater for one year, then move downstream into ocean. Mature in two to four years. From Alaska to Baja California, but rare south of Santa Cruz.

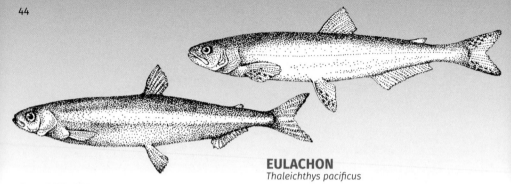

SURF SMELT
Hypomesus pretiosus

To 25 cm (10 in). Olive-green or brown above, silvery below, with bright metallic side stripe. Eats various small crustaceans and sometimes larval fish. Spawns throughout year in surf, on beaches, during the day. Females lay up to 30,000 eggs. Summer eggs hatch in 10–11 days; winter eggs take longer. A shallow-water species, surf smelts are an important food for salmon and other inshore predators. From Gulf of Alaska to Long Beach.

EULACHON
Thaleichthys pacificus

To 25 cm (10 in). Bluish-brown above, silvery with fine black speckles below. Our only smelt with lines on gill covers. Juveniles and adults eat euphausiids (shrimp-like krill) and copepods. In north, adults move into rivers to spawn March–May. Most die afterward, but some survive. Young are carried to sea by currents. An important inshore food for predators. Sometimes called candlefish because North Coast Indigenous Peoples used dried fish as candles. From Bering Sea to Monterey.

PLAINFIN MIDSHIPMAN
Porichthys notatus

To 38 cm (15 in). From light to dark brown, olive, or iridescent purple above, with yellowish belly Several rows of silver-white spots (photophores) on sides, belly, and jaw are probably used in courtship. Scaleless. Feeds at night on fish and crustaceans. Buries itself in sand/mud during day. Male scoops depression out under rock for nest (often in intertidal zone). Female fastens up to 800 eggs on overhead rock. Male survives without food, often out of water at low tide, to guard nest 16–20 days before eggs hatch. Uses gas bladder to make grunting, groaning sounds. Called "singing fish." From Sitka to Gulf of California.

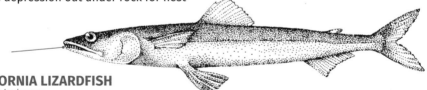

CALIFORNIA LIZARDFISH
Synodus lucioceps

To 64 cm (25 in). Brown above, lighter below, with yellowish pelvic fin. Large teeth. Eats fish. Sits on bottom, propped up on pectoral fins to wait for small fish to come within range. Young are transparent. Found on mud, sand bottom, to 25 fathoms, but some to 125 fathoms. From San Francisco to Guaymas.

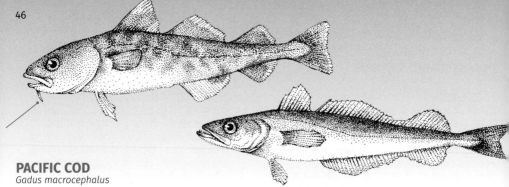

PACIFIC COD
Gadus macrocephalus

To 114 cm (45 in) with reports of larger
fish. Brown to gray above, with spots or
lighter areas on back and sides. Some fins
have white edge. Has chin barbel. Eats
worms, crabs, mollusks, shrimp, and fish.
Spawns in winter. Eggs sink, are slightly
sticky, and hatch in 8–30 days, depending
on temperature. Females mature at 40 cm,
3 years. A 60-cm female can produce over
1 million eggs. A bottom species, to 300
fathoms. Range from Bering Sea to northern
California, but some are found farther south.

PACIFIC HAKE
Merluccius productus

To 91 cm (36 in). Silver gray with black
speckles on back. Large, black mouth. Feeds
mostly at night on shrimp, sole, eulachon,
tomcods, anchovies, smelts, and other fish.
Eaten by spiny dogfish and other predators.
Spawns January–June. Eggs pelagic; float
and hatch in three days or so. Adults found
midwater to near bottom. Most to 125
fathoms; some to 500. Swims in schools.
From Alaska to Gulf of California.

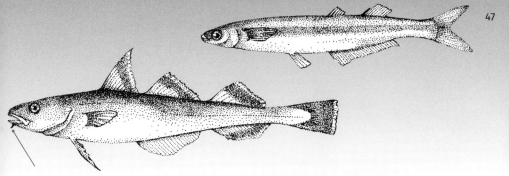

PACIFIC TOMCOD
Microgadus proximus

To 30 cm (12 in). Olive-green above, creamy-white below, with dusky fin tips. Small chin barbel. Spineless dorsal fins. Eats shrimp, probably other crustaceans. Little is known about its life history. Adults are found down to 125 fathoms, young shallower, often near surface. Over sand, mud bottom. Forms schools. A major food for large predators. Found along coast, in bays, from Bering Sea to central California.

CALIFORNIA GRUNION
Leuresthes tennis

To 19 cm (7.5 in). Greenish above, silver below, with metallic bluish side stripe. Eats small crustaceans. Spawns at night on sandy beaches, at high tide, March–September, two to six nights after full and new moons. Female wriggles backwards into sand, leaving head out, to deposit eggs in sand. Eggs hatch 15 days later. Female may spawn several times per season. An inshore fish, found down to 10 fathoms. Forms schools. From San Francisco Bay to Baja California.

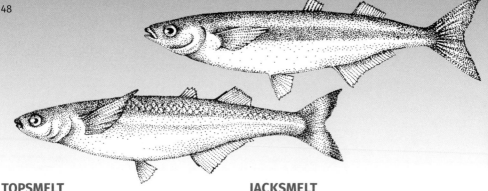

TOPSMELT
Atherinops affinis

To 37 cm (14.5 in). Green-blue above, silvery below, with metallic side stripe. Teeth small, forked. Eats small crustaceans. Forms schools March–April near entrances to bays. Spawns over shallow mudflats May–July. Sticky eggs adhere to eelgrass and kelp. Females grow faster than males. Found inshore, at surface, from British Columbia to Gulf of California.

JACKSMELT
Atherinopsis californiensis

To 44 cm (17 in). Greenish-blue above, silvery white below, with silver side stripe. Teeth not forked. Eats small crustaceans. Spawns in bays, estuaries. Eggs are sticky, forming massive grape-like clusters, and adhere to algae, eelgrass, anchor line, etc.; eaten by spiny dogfish, smoothhound sharks, and others. Jacksmelt is an important food for larger predators. Forms schools. From Oregon to Baja California.

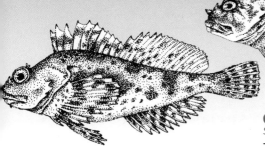

CABEZON
Scorpaenichthys marmoratus

To 99 cm (39 in). Color is variable, from reddish-olive-green to brown, with mottling. No visible scales. Body bulky. Eats fish, crabs, and abalones. Well camouflaged. Rests on bottom in crevices and on top of rocks. Spawning variable from October to March. Greenish eggs adhere to rock surface, are poisonous to humans, perhaps to other animals. A 72-cm (28-in) female is about 13 years old. Found around rocky reefs usually above 42 fathoms. From Sitka to Baja California.

RED IRISH LORD
Hemilepidotus hemilepidotus

To 51 cm (20 in) but rarely over 30 cm. Reddish, with brown, white, and black mottling. Normally have four dark saddles on back, white belly. Adults eat crabs, barnacles, mussels. Female lays masses of tough pink eggs on rocks, in spring, in intertidal or subtidal waters. From Kamchatka to Monterey. Uncommon in California, where Brown Irish Lord is more common.

STAGHORN SCULPIN
Leptocottus annatus

To 46 cm (18 in). Tan, greenish-brown, or grayish-brown, with yellow-white belly. Scaleless. Has large preopercular, antler-like spines that project outward as defense when fish is disturbed. A voracious feeder, it eats small fish, shrimp, crabs, and other invertebrates; in turn, it is eaten by striped bass, sharks, and cormorants. Spawns in winter. Common inshore over sand, mud, especially in bays, estuaries, lower reaches of coastal streams. From Bering Sea to Baja California.

GREAT SCULPIN
Myoxocephalus polyacanthocephalus

To 76 cm (30 in.) Back is deep olive color with four dark saddles. Brown bars on fins. Long, straight, smooth preopercular spine. Eats small fish, crabs, and other invertebrates. Little is known about its life history. Common on shallow reefs from Bering Sea to Washington.

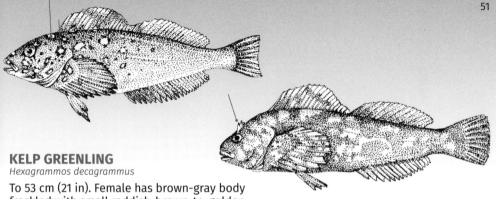

KELP GREENLING
Hexagrammos decagrammus

To 53 cm (21 in). Female has brown-gray body freckled with small reddish-brown-to-golden spots. Male has gray-to-brownish-olive body with irregular blue spots. Yellow-orange fins, yellowish mouth. Kelp greenling eats small fish, shrimp, decorator crabs, octopi, and worms. Spawns October–November. Female lays large masses of pale-blue eggs; male guards nest. Young are eaten by steelhead, salmon. Found in rocky inshore areas, on the bottom. From Aleutian Islands to southern California, but rare in south.

ROCK GREENLING
Hexagrammos lagocephalus

To 61 cm (24 in). Greenish to brown with dark mottling. Mouth bluish. Two red lines radiate back and down from eye. Males have large red blotches on sides. Rock greenling eats worms, shrimp, crabs, and small fish. Reproduction similar to kelp greenling. Common in shallow, rocky areas and along exposed coasts. From Bering Sea to Point Conception.

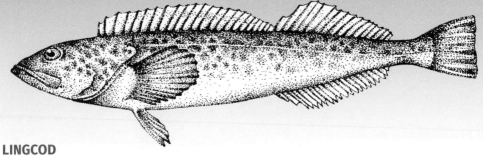

LINGCOD
Ophiodon elongatus

To 152 cm (60 in), some to 70 lbs. Mottled
gray, brown, green, or bluish. Large mouth
and canine-like teeth. Small scales.
Lingcod is an aggressive, voracious predator,
eating mostly other fish. Moves into shallow
water in fall or early winter to spawn. Male
guards nest of eggs attached to rocks.
Young are found on sand or mud bottom in
bays and inshore areas, adults down to 233
fathoms. From Kodiak Island to northern
Baja California.

ROCKFISH BIOLOGY

Rockfish, or rockcod, are a common, diversified, and popular group, with over 60 species along the Pacific Coast. They have large mouths, bright colors, choice flesh, and large erectable dorsal spines that cause painful wounds to careless handlers. Their dorsal, anal, and pelvic fin spines lack venom glands, but the slimy material around the spines can cause prolonged irritation and pain in puncture wounds.

Rockfish are major predators. While some species feed on macroplankton, such as euphausiid shrimp and hyperiid amphipods, others eat fish, various crabs, worms, shrimp, and even small shark pups.

The reproductive cycle is quick. Eggs develop in about one month after internal fertilization. The large females of some species may contain up to 2 million eggs. The eggs hatch into tiny larvae (3–5 mm long) as they contact sea water. Rockfish larvae are pelagic, plankton eaters. When they reach 50 mm in length, most move inshore and stay close to or on hard substrates, from tidepools to 17 fathoms. Some adults live to over 300 fathoms. Color changes with growth.

Rockfish are highly territorial and will defend their space against other rockfish intruders. They are often found in close proximity to each other, indicating territories may be both small and seasonal. Rockfish also have strong attachment to a homesite. One study showed that yellowtail rockfish, tagged and removed up to 14 miles, returned to their exact homesite. Most stay close to their homesite areas. No migration has been observed for inshore species. When caught and suddenly brought to the surface, reduced external pressure greatly expands the swim bladder and makes the eyes bulge and stomach protrude from the mouth.

COPPER ROCKFISH
Sebastes caurinus

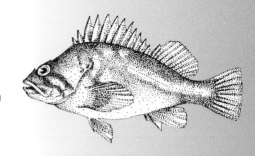

To 56 cm (22 in). Color is highly variable: orange-brown, olive, dull yellow, copper, or reddish. Posterior section of lateral line is usually whitish or pink with white blotches. Two copper-orange bars usually angle down from eyes toward gills or pectoral fins. Eats other fish, crabs, shrimp. Found over rocky bottom down to 100 fathoms. From Alaska to central Baja California.

CALICO ROCKFISH
Sebastes dallii

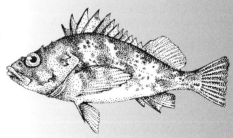

To 25 cm (10 in). Broad, oblique bars on sides with irregular brown blotches. Overall color is yellowish-green, with brown-to-red-brown streaks and spots on caudal fin. Eats fish and crustaceans. Found on or over sand or mud bottom down to 140 fathoms. From San Francisco to central Baja California, but rare north of Santa Barbara.

TREEFISH
Sebastes serriceps

To 41 cm (16 in). Adults have five to six thick, black bars on an olive-yellow body, with red-pink lips. Young have a more yellow body, without the pink-red lips. Found around shallow rock reefs with caves and crevices to 25 fathoms. Solitary and highly territorial. From San Francisco to central Baja California, but rare north of Santa Barbara.

TIGER ROCKFISH
Sebastes nigrocinctus

To 61 cm (24 in). Pink-to-red body has five black or dark-red bars, with four bars radiating from eyes. Adult sometimes has spots between bars. Anal and pelvic fins black-tipped in young. Found on rocky reefs down to 150 fathoms. Solitary. Very aggressive in defending territory. From Alaska to central California.

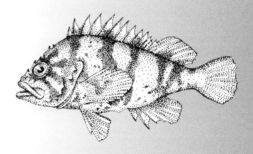

FLAG ROCKFISH
Sebastes rubrivinctus

To 51 cm (20 in). Pinkish or pure white, with broad red or reddish-black bars. First red bar angles down from first dorsal spine across gill cover. Found on rocky reefs and over sand bottom down to 100 fathoms. From San Francisco to Baja California. Closely resembles redbanded rockfish.

REDBANDED ROCKFISH
Sebastes babcocki

To 64 cm (25 in). Pinkish-white, with four broad red or reddish-black bars. First red bar starts in front of dorsal fin, touches upper edge of gill cover, and ends on the pectoral fin. Young born April–May. Half of males are mature at 38 cm, females at 42 cm (British Columbia). Found over sandy bottom, to 50 fathoms in north and 340 fathoms in south. From Aleutian Islands to San Diego, but uncommon south of San Francisco.

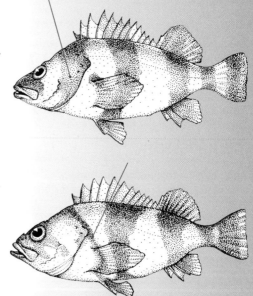

CHINA ROCKFISH
Sebastes nebulosus

To 43 cm (17 in). Black to blue-black, mottled with yellow-white spots. A broad yellow stripe runs from third or fourth spine of dorsal fin down to and along lateral line to tail. Some blue around face, fins. Pronounced head spines. Eats crabs, shrimp, brittle stars, small fish. Solitary. Found mostly in or near rock crevices or caves to 70 fathoms. From Alaska to San Miguel Island.

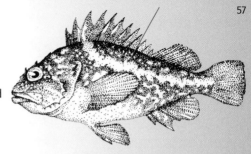

BLACK AND YELLOW ROCKFISH
Sebastes chrysomelas

To 39 cm (15 in). Black to olive-brown, with large irregular yellow blotches and spots. Yellow on third and seventh dorsal fin spines. Found close to rocks, crevices, caves, intertidal zone to 20 fathoms. From Eureka to Baja California.

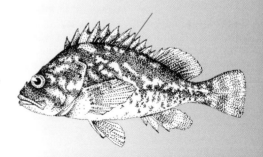

GOPHER ROCKFISH
Sebastes carnatus

To 39 cm (15 in). Brown to olive, mottled with pink to whitish blotches and spots. Yellow-orange lower lip. Eats crabs, squid, and small fish. Found in shallow, rocky areas down to 30 fathoms. From Eureka to Baja California. Closely resembles black and yellow rockfish.

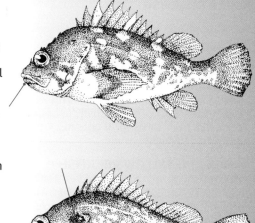

BROWN ROCKFISH
Sebastes auriculatus

To 55 cm (21 in). Light brown with dark-brown mottling and dark-brown blotch at top of gill cover. Belly pinkish. Females, 31 cm long, can produce about 339,000 eggs per season. Born in June (Puget Sound area). Widely distributed in shallow water, in bays, near shore, also to 70 fathoms offshore. Most common rockfish in San Francisco Bay. From Alaska to Baja California.

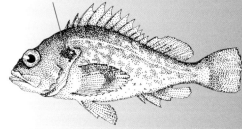

GRASS ROCKFISH
Sebastes rastrelliger

To 56 cm (22 in). Dark green to olive, mottled with light green, gray on sides. Lower pectoral fin rays pinkish in some adults. Thick body. Common in rocky areas, along jetties, in kelp and eelgrass. Usually found in less than 9 fathoms, but occasionally to 25 fathoms. From Oregon to Baja California.

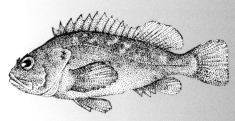

KELP ROCKFISH
Sebastes atrovirens

To 42 cm (16 in). Olive-brown to gray-brown with dark-brown mottling. Belly sometimes pinkish. A solitary fish usually found off the bottom, suspended midwater near kelp, or resting on it, to 45 fathoms. From Sonoma County to central Baja California.

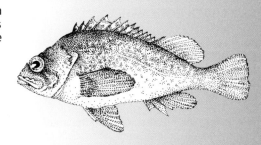

GREEN SPOTTED ROCKFISH
Sebastes chlorostictus

To 50 cm (19 in). Body yellowish-pink with many roundish bright-green spots and three to five large white-to-pink blotches on back. Fins pink with yellow on membranes. Found on sand or mud bottom to 110 fathoms. From Copalis Head to central Baja California.

Greenblotched rockfish *(S. rosenblatti)* has green wavy lines in circles, but not in spots.

QUILLBACK ROCKFISH
Sebastes maliger

To 61 cm (24 in). Brown to blackish or brown and light yellow with large mottled orange areas, particularly about head, face, and back. Membrane between dorsal spines deeply incised. Found around rocky reefs, caves, and crevices. A common, solitary, inshore rockfish in the north. In the south, found down to 150 fathoms. From Gulf of Alaska to southern California.

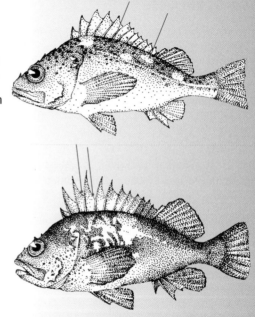

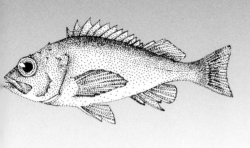

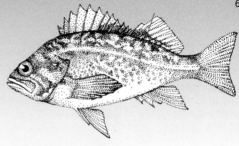

STRIPETAIL ROCKFISH
Sebastes saxicola

To 41 cm (16 in). Body pinkish-red to yellowish-pink with traces of green or dusky saddles on back. Green stripes on caudal fin sometimes faint. Young born 4 mm long, in February (British Columbia). Some mature at 2 years and 12.7 cm. Half of the males are mature at 14.6 cm (California). Females mature after reaching 17 cm and can release 15,000–230,000 eggs. Found offshore on sand or mud bottom to 308 fathoms; common below 17 fathoms. From southern Alaska to central Baja California.

CANARY ROCKFISH
Sebastes pinniger

To 76 cm (30 in). Orange, with gray blotches. Lateral line usually in a clear gray area. Fins bright orange. Head usually with three bright-orange stripes radiating from eye. Dark blotch at end of spiny rays. Eats small fish and krill. Young are born in January (British Columbia). Half the population matures at 35.6 cm (14 in), 5 to 6 years old (California). Females carry 260,000–1.9 million eggs. Found over rocky bottoms to 241 fathoms. From southern Alaska to northern Baja California.

VERMILION ROCKFISH
Sebastes miniatus

To 76 cm (30 in). Has reddish back mottled with gray, red-orange sides and belly, and red fins, often with dark edges. Orange stripes radiate from eyes. Most of lateral line gray to white. Deep-water specimens are more reddish; shallow water specimens are more brownish overall. Found on shallow-to-deep rocky reefs. More abundant in shallow water, but found to 240 fathoms. From Queen Charlotte Islands to Baja California.

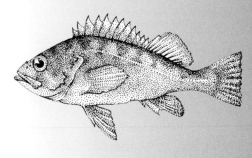

BRONZESPOTTED ROCKFISH
Sebastes gilli

To 71 cm (28 in). Reddish-orange with two bright, clear orange areas below soft dorsal fin. Roundish bronze or brown spots on back and upper sides. Lateral line in a narrow red zone. Brown bars radiate from eyes. Upturned mouth. Common in deep water in southern California to 205 fathoms. From Monterey to northern Baja California.

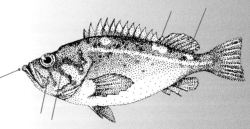

OLIVE ROCKFISH
Sebastes serrandides

To 61 cm (24 in). Olive-brown above, pale below lateral line, with pale blotches along upper back, below dorsal fin. Fins olive, sometimes yellowish. Has nine rays in caudal fin. Eats mainly fish, squid, and sometimes plankton. Found over rocky reefs and in clear, quiet kelp beds, usually above 17 fathoms, but occasionally to 80 fathoms. From northern California to central Baja California. Closely resembles yellowtail rockfish and kelp bass.

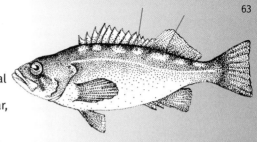

STARRY ROCKFISH
Sebastes constellatus

To 46 cm (18 in). Red-orange with three to five large white blotches on back and many small dots over body. Usually found on deep rocky reefs and in caves and crevices to 150 fathoms. From San Francisco to southern Baja California.

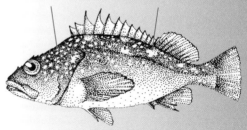

ROSY ROCKFISH
Sebastes rosaceus

To 36 cm (14 in), but rarely over 28 cm
(11 in). Red-purple mottling on back, often
with irregular patches of purple. Four to five
white blotches ringed by purple on back. One
to two purple bars radiate from eyes. Fins
orange-red, membranes greenish-yellow.
Found around caves, crevices on rocky reefs,
to 70 fathoms, but usually shallower. From
Puget Sound to central Baja California, but
rare north of California.

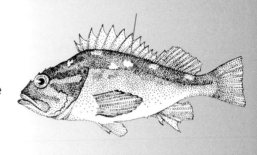

BLACKGILL ROCKFISH
Sebastes melanostomus

To 61 cm (24 in). Dark red with black on rear
edge of gill cover. Inside of mouth is mostly
black. Fins red. A deep-water species, found
to 420 fathoms, but young are found in
shallower water. Over sand or mud bottom,
from Washington to central Baja California.

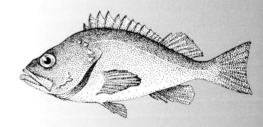

BOCACCIO
Sebastes paucispinis

To 91 cm (36 in). Olive-brown to red above; silvery pink on sides. Young have brown spots on sides. Mouth large; lower jaw projects. Adults are voracious carnivores that eat mostly other fish, including rockfish. Lives to 50 years or more. Half are mature at 42 cm or four years (California). Eggs released October–July. Young are 4–6 mm at birth and feed near surface. Adults are found over rocky reefs and sand or mud bottom, to 263 fathoms, but most above 137 fathoms. Wide-ranging, from Kodiak Island to central Baja California.

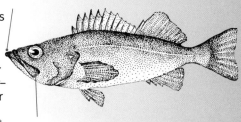

CHILIPEPPER
Sebastes goodei

To 56 cm (22 in). Mostly reddish-pink above, white below. White lateral line in a clear pink or red zone. Fins pink; soft dorsal and caudal fins dusky. Eats krill, small fish, and squid. Half of males are mature at 29 cm. Found over deep rocky reefs and sand or mud bottom to 180 fathoms. From Vancouver Island to southern Baja California.

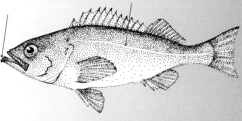

YELLOWEYE ROCKFISH *Sebastes ruberrimus*
To 91 cm (36 in). Specimens up to 30 cm are orange to reddish with a white stripe along lateral line and onto head with a shorter second stripe below; black on pectoral, anal, and caudal fins. Larger specimens are more orange and lack lower stripe; lateral stripe may be pale. Eye bright yellow. Young born in June (Washington). Lives on rocky reefs to 300 fathoms. From Gulf of Alaska to northern Baja California.

COWCOD *Sebastes levis*
To 94 cm (37 in), 28 lbs. Mostly pinkish-red with four to five narrow, dusky, irregular vertical bars. Young have black spots near bars. In large specimens, the spine membranes of the dorsal fin are deeply notched. Eats fish, octopi, and squid. Large females spawn over 2 million eggs or larvae, in winter or early spring. Adults are found on rocky bottom less than 100 fathoms. From Mendocino to Baja California.

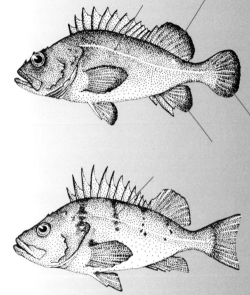

BLACK ROCKFISH *Sebastes melanops*

To 60 cm (24 in). Black or blue-black, mottled with gray. Some specimens have light patches on back and gray stripe along lateral line. Dark spots on dorsal fin. Upper jaw extends beneath and behind eye. Eats fish, squid, and shrimp. Found on or over rocky bottom, sometimes over sand, from surface to 200 fathoms. Sometimes forms schools. From Amchitka Island to San Miguel Island.

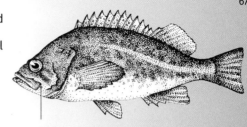

BLUE ROCKFISH *Sebastes mystinus*

To 53 cm (21 in). Dark blue, mottled with light blue. No spots on dorsal fin. Upper jaw reaches eye but does not extend past it. Young are gray with red streaks and black spots; born in winter. They frequent offshore kelp beds in northern California and are prey to ospreys (fish hawks). Blue rockfish eats large planktonic animals, jellyfish, salps, algae, and small fish. Adults are usually found well above shallow or deep rocky reefs, in or near kelp beds, at surface to 300 fathoms. Forms schools. From Bering Sea to Punta Banda.

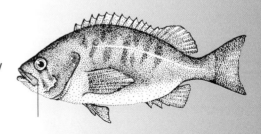

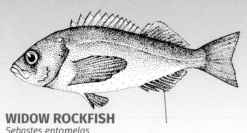

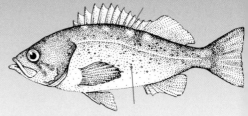

WIDOW ROCKFISH
Sebastes entomelas

To 53 cm (21 in). Dusky, brassy brown above, with some yellow; light below. Spiny dorsal fin light; other fins dark. Small specimens have faint orange streaks. Black membranes between rays of anal, pelvic, and pectoral fins. Young eat plankton. Adults eat macroplankton, particularly hyperiid amphipods, and sometimes small squid and anchovies. Half mature at four years, 32 cm. Widow rockfish forms large schools, midwater, over rocky or sandy bottom. Found from surface to 200 fathoms. From Kodiak Island to Baja California.

YELLOWTAIL ROCKFISH
Sebastes flavidus

To 66 cm (26 in). Olive, greenish-brown, or dark gray, with light areas, on back, and pale below. Red-orange-brown speckles on scales. Caudal fin dirty yellow; other fins may be yellow. Separated from look-alike olive rockfish by two yellow areas on gill cover, eight soft rays in caudal fin, and speckles on scales. Eats small hake, anchovies, lantern fish, euphausiid shrimp, and small squid. Young born January–February (Oregon). May live to 64 years. Yellowtail have a strong homing instinct (see p. 53). Mostly pelagic, over deep reefs, in schools, most commonly surface to 100 fathoms. From Kodiak Island to southern California.

SURFPERCH BIOLOGY

Surfperch are one of the most commonly encountered inshore fish along the Pacific Coast. Most are brightly colored, with some silver, and often barred or striped. Breeding males or females may be much more intense in color. Their bodies often seem laterally compressed, presenting a narrow form head on. Most species propel themselves with downward thrusts of the pectoral fins in a slightly jerky, up-and-down motion.

Surperch eat a variety of large zooplankton, invertebrates, and some algae. Special grinding teeth in the backs of their mouths allow some species to crush small mussel and clam shells to digest the flesh inside. Some species act as cleaner fish, picking parasites off of other fish.

Fertilization is internal. Males use the thickened front part of the anal fin to inject sperm, but fertilization of eggs often occurs months after copulation. Surfperch are **vivaparous.** Young are born alive, often at 30–40 mm, after a gestation period of several months. Developing embryos inside the mother use their highly vascular fins to absorb nourishment and oxygen. Litters are usually less than 10, but large females may bear up to 60. Some males are sexually active right after birth. Females mature a year or so later. Lifespan can range from 3 years for shiner surfperch to over 9 years for black surfperch.

Surfperch are found in surf, kelp beds, on rocky reefs, in bays, estuaries, near piers, jetties, and in tidepools. There are 21 species of surfperch, all limited to the Northern Pacific region. Along our coast, 18 are marine, one of which, the shiner surfperch, enters freshwater. Another surfperch, the tule perch, is restricted to freshwater along our coast. Two species live off Japan and Korea.

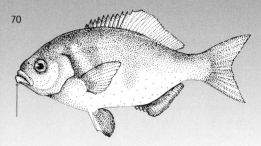
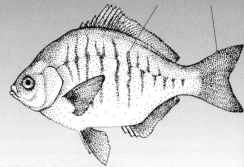

RUBBERLIP SURFPERCH, RUBBERLIP SEAPERCH
Rhacochilus toxotes

To 47 cm (18.5 in). Our largest surfperch is silvery olive, fading to brassy yellow below. Has thick white or pink lips and yellow pectoral fins. First ray of soft dorsal fin shorter than third ray. Spiny rays shorter than soft rays of dorsal fin. Eats shrimp, amphipods, and small crabs. Bears young in spring; 20 or more per female. Often forms schools. Found in quiet waters of harbors and bays, around piers and kelp beds, and outside the surf on open coast. Surface to 25 fathoms. From Mendocino to Baja California.

REDTAIL SURFPERCH
Amphistichus rhodoterus

To 41 cm (16 in). Body is brassy silver with olive tinge along back and 8–11 reddish-brown bars on sides. All fins, especially caudal, are red. Spiny rays of dorsal fin higher than soft rays. Redtail surfperch eats sand-dwelling crustaceans (mole crabs, amphipods) and mollusks, along steeply sloping sandy beaches. Found in surf, and down to 4 fathoms; sometimes seen in bays, sloughs, and backwaters. From Vancouver Island to Monterey Bay. The most common surfperch caught in surf from central California north.

BARRED SURFPERCH
Amphistichus argenteus

To 43 cm (17 in). Silvery to brassy olive; back is marked with blue or gray. Has 8–10 somewhat irregular brassy gold bars on side with spots in between. Eats mostly sand crabs but also bean clams and small amphipods. Mates in fall or early winter. Specimens over 25 cm long usually have 45 or so young born March–July. Females grow older and larger than males. Barred surfperch is most abundant in surf along sandy, open ocean beaches. Some found to 40 fathoms. From Bodega Bay to Baja California.

CALICO SURFPERCH
Amphistichus koelzi

To 30 cm (12 in). Silvery blue to brassy or olive. Sides have reddish-to-brownish bars made up of small spots broken by a lateral line. Fins reddish; caudal fin dusky. Calico surfperch is common in surf of sandy beaches and to 5 fathoms. From Cape Flattery to northern Baja California, but rare north of California.

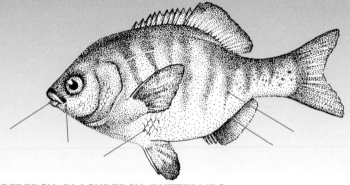

BLACK SURFPERCH, BLACKPERCH, BUTTERLIPS
Embiotoca jacksoni

To 39 cm (15.5 in). Color varies, but overall is usually dark rusty brown, with up to nine vertical bars on side. Orange-to-yellow-orange lips with a dark "moustache." Blue specks on scales and blue bar at base of anal fin. Has a noticeable patch of enlarged scales below pectoral fin. Eats worms, crustaceans, mollusks, and small fish. Some black surfperch act as cleaners, picking parasites off of other fish and their own kind. Found over rocky areas near kelp; sometimes over sand or mud bottom of bays, around piers or pilings. In San Francisco Bay, it's associated with oyster- or mussel-shell bottom with Gigartina kelp. Forms schools. Found from surface to 40 fathoms. From Fort Bragg to Baja California.

WALLEYE SURFPERCH
Hyperprosopon argenteum

To 30 cm (12 in). Highly compressed body is silver, often bluish above, sometimes with faint pinkish bars. Large eyes and striking black edge on pelvic fins are key features. Dark-edged caudal and anal fins; breeding females have dark anal fins. Breeding males are darker overall. Eats small crustaceans. Breeds October–December; 5–12 young born in spring. Found in surf; over sand or mud bottom; over rock reefs, kelp, and around piers. Bays and outer coast to 100 fathoms. From Vancouver Island to Baja California.

SILVER SURFPERCH
Hyperprosopon ellipticum

To 27 cm (10.5 in) but usually smaller. Silver-gray to greenish above, silver below; may have faint dusky bars on sides. Caudal fin pinkish. Anal fin usually with a black or orange spot. Dorsal and caudal fins may have dark edge. Found in surf, over sandy areas, around rocks and piers to 60 fathoms. From British Columbia to northern Baja California.

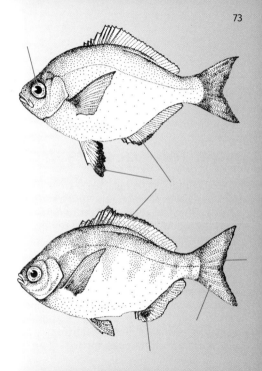

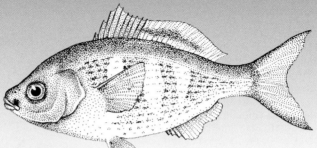

SHINER SURFPERCH, SHINER PERCH
Cymatogaster aggregata

To 18 cm (7 in) but usually 10–13 cm (4–5 in). Silvery with rows of dark spots, forming stripes. (This feature is exaggerated in breeding males.) Stripes are crossed by three yellow bars, which are less noticeable in males in summer. A dark spot above corner of mouth is often present. Eats zooplankton, small crustaceans, algae, mussels, and barnacles. Sexes tend to be separate, except during summer breeding season. Male courtship includes elaborate display involving fin nipping, darting back and forth, and appearing to isolate selected female. Sperm is stored in ovarian compartment five to six months before eggs are fertilized. In spring, females move over intertidal mudflats in San Francisco Bay at high tide to bear up to 36 young per litter. Males are mature at birth. Females give birth in their second year. Found around eelgrass, piers, pilings of bays, sloughs, in calm areas of exposed coast. Enters freshwater rivers. Usually in shallow water, but known to 80 fathoms. Forms loose schools. From southern Alaska to northern Baja California.

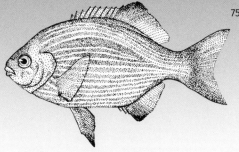

RAINBOW SURFPERCH, RAINBOW SEAPERCH
Hypsurus caryi

To 30 cm (12 in). Body has orange-and-blue horizontal stripes and orange bars on back. Blue spots and streaks on head. Black spot near corner of upper lip. Pelvic fins bright orange with whitish-blue edge, but soft dorsal and anal fins have dark blotches. Belly flat but may turn upward in front of anal fin. Some rainbow surfperch act as cleaners, picking parasites off of other fish. Found over rocky bottom, along edges of kelp beds, and occasionally over sand, but not in surf. To 22 fathoms. Forms schools in the fall for breeding. From Cape Mendocino to northern Baja California.

STRIPED SURFPERCH, STRIPED SEAPERCH
Embiotoca lateralis

To 38 cm (15 in). Body has 15 or so horizontal reddish-orange-and-blue stripes below lateral line. Stripes are curved above lateral line. Blue spots and streaks on head and operculum. Upper lip often black. Pelvic fins dusky. Eats small crustaceans, worms, mussels, and herring eggs. Up to 44 young per litter are born in June or July (British Columbia). Found over reefs, in kelp beds and bays, around piers. Offshore to 12 fathoms. From southern Alaska to Baja California.

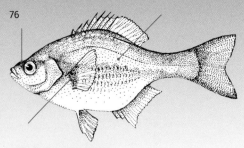

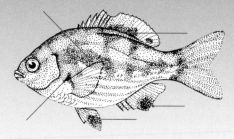

KELP SURFPERCH
Brachyistius frenatus

To 22 cm (8.5 in). Brassy to golden brown; dark above, sometimes with blue spots or streaks; paler and often reddish below. Fins plain, sometimes rosy. Black specks on upper pectoral. Sharp upturned snout and oblique mouth. Short dorsal fin with large space to caudal. Eats seaweed isopods and other kelp-associated crustaceans. Picks parasites off of other fish. Forms schools in summer for breeding. Matures in first year (California). Rarely found far from kelp. At surface to 15 fathoms. From southern British Columbia to central Baja California.

DWARF SURFPERCH, DWARFPERCH
Micrometrus minimus

Less than 7.6 cm (3 in). Silver-blue, greenish to olive on back; yellow, green-silver below; large, irregular dark stripe on side, crossed by dark bars. Black triangle at base of pectoral fin. Dorsal, anal, pelvic fins have black blotches. Eats algae and small invertebrates. Found in rocky inshore areas, around seaweed and tidepools, to 5 fathoms. From Bodega Bay to central Baja California.

REEF SURFPERCH, REEFPERCH
Micrometrus aurora

To 18 cm (7 in). Blue-greenish above, fading to silver below, often with orange-gold stripe from pectoral to near caudal fin. Scales between anal and pectoral fins are black-edged. Black triangular blotch at base of pectoral. Eats algae and small invertebrates. Found in shallow rocky areas, tidepools, to 3.3 fathoms. From Tomales Bay to north-central Baja California.

WHITE SURFPERCH, WHITE SEAPERCH
Phanerodon furcatus

To 32 cm (12.5 in). Body is silver, bluish to olive above, silver below (may have yellowish-to-rosy tint). Fins yellowish, with black line at base of dorsal fin, sometimes a black spot on front edge of anal fin. White surfperch are usually found near piers, in bays, sandy areas, quiet water, and offshore rocks to 24 fathoms. From Vancouver Island to northern Baja California.

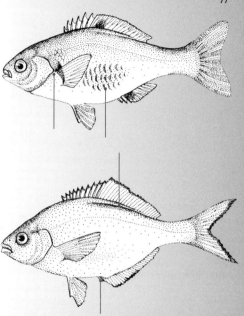

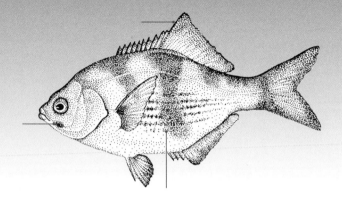

PILE SURFPERCH, PILEPERCH
Rhacochilus vacca

To 44 cm (17.5 in). Blackish-gray to brownish above, silvery below, usually with a broad vertical dark bar at midside. Often a dark spot below eye. Breeding males are quite dark. Caudal fin deeply forked. Soft rays taller than spiny rays. Eats various mussels, small clams, barnacles, and shrimp. Mates in late summer or fall; fertilization of eggs delayed until December–February. Young born mostly July–August, with up to 61 per litter (Oregon). Found on rocky shores, kelp beds, and pilings; common in bays and estuaries.

To 40 fathoms. From southern Alaska to north-central Baja California.

STRIPED BASS
Morone saxatilis

To 122 cm (48 in), 90lbs. Greenish-black; silver sides with six to nine black stripes on scale rows; white belly. Anadromous, moving regularly between salt and freshwater. lives mostly in or near estuaries. Adults eat various fish, including young stripers. Larvae feed on plankton, copepods, and mysid shrimp. Adults move into freshwater in fall and stay until spring when they spawn at the surface in open river water. After spawning, adults return to San Francisco Bay or the ocean. Males mature at 2 to 3 years, females at 5 to 6 years.

Striped bass are native to the East Coast. Over 430 stripers were introduced in San Francisco Bay and the delta in 1879 and 1882. By 1899, stripers had dispersed to below the Mexico border and up to British Columbia. Largest population was in San Francisco Bay. This popular sport fish saw serious population declines in the 1960s, followed by a rebound in the late 1990s. and a decline again in recent years. The causes of the original decline were likely related to water use changes in California, and today they are also threatened by an illegal black market as well.

(See illustration on page 80.)

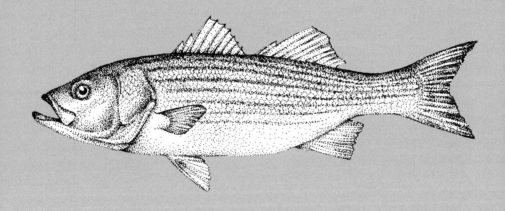

SPOTTED SAND BASS
Paralabrax maculatofasciatus

To 56 cm (22 in). Olive-brown above, pale below, with round black spots on fins and body, broad faint bars on back. Young have dark stripes. Eats crabs, shrimp, and fish. Found on sand or mud bottom, near rocks, in eelgrass, to 33 fathoms. From Monterey to Mazatlan.

KELP BASS
Paralabrax clathratus

To 72 cm (28.5 in). Olive-brown above, cream below, with pale blotches on back, yellowish tinge on fins. Breeding males have orange chin and lower jaw. Eats crabs, shrimp, squid, octopi, worms, and fish. Spawns from late spring to fall. This slow-growing fish occurs around reefs, wrecks, and kelp beds, to 25 fathoms. From mouth of Columbia River to Bahia Magdalena, but most abundant in southern California.

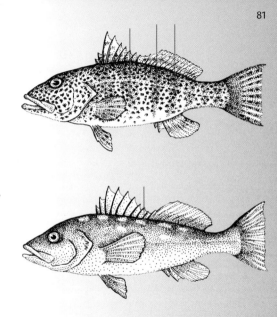

BARRED SAND BASS
Paralabrax nebulifer

To 65 cm (25.5 in). Gray, greenish-brown above, with dark bars on side, pale below; gold-brown, orange spots on head. Third dorsal spine is long. Eats crabs, shrimp, and fish. Usually found over sand bottom, sometimes near or among rocks, to 100 fathoms. From Santa Cruz to southern Baja California.

WHITE SEA BASS
Atractoscion nobilis

To 152 cm (60 in). Adults are gray-blue to copper above, silvery white below, with dark spots and black spot at base of pectoral. Young, to 61 cm, have three to six dusky bars on sides and yellowish fins. Eats fish and squid. Congregates inshore April–August to spawn. All mature at 75 cm. Found in schools over rocky bottom or in kelp beds, to 67 fathoms. From Juneau to southern Baja California, but rare north of California. This species is a croaker and not related to preceding bass.

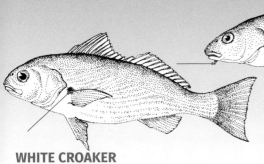

WHITE CROAKER
Genyonemus lineatus

To 41 cm (16 in) but usually less than 30 cm. Brassy silver above with dark specks, pale below with a hint of wavy lines along scale rows. Caudal fin dark-edged, other fins yellow-white. Has small black spot at top of pectoral fin base. Produces croaking noise with swim bladder. Eats various bottom invertebrates. Matures at 13–15 cm. Spawns November–May. Forms schools. Most are found inshore, to 17 fathoms, but some to 130 fathoms. From British Columbia to southern Baja California, but rare north of California.

CALIFORNIA CORBINA
Menticirrhus undulatus

To 71 cm (28 in). Dark gray, blue on back, white belly; may have light and dark oblique streaks. Single, short chin barbel. Pectoral fin black. Swim bladder absent; can't make sounds like other croakers. Adults eat sand crabs, small shrimp, bean clams, and worms. Spawning occurs offshore June–September, but mostly July and August. Usually found in small groups, but large fish are solitary. Some migrate 50 miles. Almost always over sand or mud bottom on open coast or in bays, sloughs. To 11 fathoms. Commonly caught by surf and pier fishermen in southern California. From Point Conception to Gulf of California.

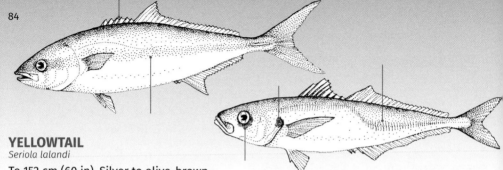

YELLOWTAIL
Seriola lalandi

To 152 cm (60 in). Silver to olive-brown above, silvery below, with broad yellow stripe head to tail. Fins, particularly caudal, yellow. Eats anchovies, sardines, mackerel, squid, and pelagic red crabs. Acts as a cleaner fish, picking parasites off of blue sharks. Many spawn at 2 years old, nearly all at 3 years, June–October, but July and August are peak months. Most spawn off central and southern Baja California. Found around offshore banks and islands, kelp beds, and rocky areas, to 160 fathoms, but at surface in summer. Forms schools. From British Columbia to Chile.

JACK MACKEREL
Tracburus symmetricus

To 81 cm (32 in). Metallic blue to olive-green, sometimes mottled above, silver below. Dark under eye, dark spot on gill cover. Lateral line dips sharply behind pectoral fin. Caudal fin has yellow-red tones. Eats mainly microplankton but also lanternfish, sauries, and squid. Most are mature at 3 years, 31 cm. Spawns February–May in middle of night. Eggs near surface. Fish pelagic, at surface to 219 fathoms, in large schools. From southern Alaska to southern Baja California.

GARIBALDI
Hypsypops rubicundus

To 36 cm (14 in). Adult is solid bright orange, with green eyes. Young Garibaldi is red-orange or brick-red with iridescent blue spots/blotches. Eats mostly attached invertebrates. Propels itself with pectoral fins. Spawns March–July. Male clears sheltered rock of all growth prior to spawning. Female deposits eggs; male fertilizes them and stubbornly guards nest against intruders. Adult defends home territory and, when disturbed, produces thumping sounds. Found over reefs, in kelp beds, to 16 fathoms. From Monterey to southern Baja California, but rare north of Point Conception. **CAUTION: This fish is protected by law from all forms of collecting. PLEASE RELEASE UNHARMED.**

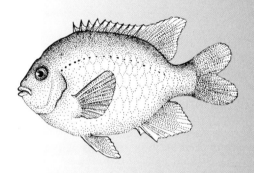

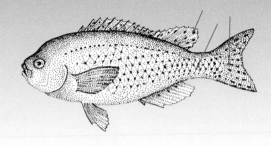

BLACKSMITH
Chromis punctipinnis

To 30 cm (12 in) but usually smaller. Gray-blue with black spots on rear part of body, soft dorsal, and caudal fins. Young are purple in front, yellow at rear. Young pick parasites off of other fish. Spawns in summer. Male cleans nest site, herds female to it, then guards eggs until they hatch. Found on reefs, kelp beds, to 45 fathoms. From Monterey to central Baja California, but rare north of Point Conception.

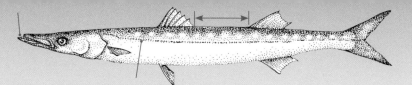

CALIFORNIA BARRACUDA, PACIFIC BARRACUDA *Sphyraena argentea*

To 122 cm (48 in). Brown to blue above, silver below. Caudal fin yellow. Some have oblique bars on back. Has strong jaws and large teeth. Eats mostly other fish. Most are mature at 2 years. Spawns in summer. Female may spawn several times per season. Eggs are pelagic. This schooling species lives inshore to 10 fathoms. Migrates north in summer, south in autumn. Although highly esteemed for edible flesh, some are occasionally toxic. From Kodiak Island to southern Baja California, but rare north of Morro Bay.

WOLF-EEL, WOLF FISH *Anarrhichthys ocellatus*

To 203 cm (81.5 in). Gray to brown, sometimes greenish, with light rings around dark spots over body and fins. Young often orange. Has pudgy, wrinkled, old man–like face and large canine teeth. Eats crabs, urchins, and fish. Spawns in winter months. Deposits eggs on rocky surface in large mass, which both parents guard until hatching. Found in and around rock reefs to 123 fathoms. From Aleutian Islands to southern California. Not a true eel.

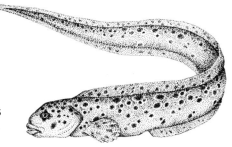

CALIFORNIA SHEEPHEAD
Semicossyphus pulcher

To 91 cm (36 in). Male has black head; red eye; red, pink, or dusky red midbody; and blackish rear. Female is solid rose to red-brown. Both sexes have white chins. Young are red-orange with a white side stripe. Most fins have large black blotch. Older male may have large bump on head. Large teeth protrude from mouth. Eats urchins, scallops, lobsters, crabs, and abalones. All are female until they reach 30 cm, then change into males. Spawn in spring or summer. Eggs are free-floating. Adults may live 50 years. Found on rock reefs, in kelp forests, to 48 fathoms. From Monterey to Cabo San Lucas.

SENORITA
Oxyjulus californica

To 25 cm (10 in). Dusky yellow overall; often orangish-brown above, pale below. Caudal fin has large black area. Eats small snails, crabs, isopods, worms, and larval fish. May pick parasites off of other fish. Spawns May–August. Matures at 1 year. Often buries itself in sand at night to sleep with head protruding. Found on rocky reefs, in kelp beds, to 55 fathoms. From Salt Point, Sonoma County, to Cedros Island.

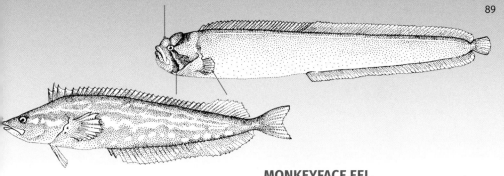

GIANT KELPFISH
Heterostichus rostratus

To 61 cm (24 in). Usually yellowish-brown to green and purple with light mottling, sometimes with silver stripes or irregular bars. Color pattern matches surrounding algae. Hard for divers to see. Eats small crustaceans, mollusks, and fishes. Giant kelpfish is usually found resting on or among kelp blades, among algae-covered rocks, or in eelgrass, to 22 fathoms. From British Columbia to Cabo San Lucas.

MONKEYFACE EEL, MONKEYFACE PRICKLEBACK
Cebidichthys violaceus

To 76 cm (30 in). Usually solid olive, gray, or black with two dark streaks radiating down from eye. May have orange spots on body and orange edges on fins. Adult has lumpy ridge on top of head. No pelvic fins. Eats crabs, shrimp, isopods, and algae. Lays eggs on rocks and guards them until hatching. Found inshore in crevices of rocky areas, tidepools, to 13 fathoms. From southern Oregon to north-central Baja California.

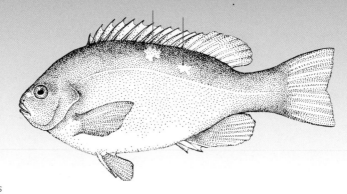

OPALEYE
Cirella nigricans

To 66 cm (27 in). Olive-green-to-gray-green body with two light spots on back. Large specimens may not show these spots. May have a white bar across head between eyes. Eats seaweed and eelgrass. One theory suggests it gets its nourishment from the invertebrates on the algae. Spawns April–June. Reaches maturity in two to three years. Found on shallow reefs and in kelp beds, to 16 fathoms. From San Francisco to Cabo San Lucas.

TUNA BIOLOGY

Pacific mackerel, skipjack, bonito, albacore, yellowfin, and bluefin tuna are closely related members of the mackerel family, known collectively as tuna. They occur in tropical, temperate, and cold seas, and often make long migrations. One tagged albacore migrated 4,900 miles in 11 months.

Tuna tend to be nearly scaleless, heavily muscled, torpedo-shaped, and fast. Their dorsal fins can fold into grooves to minimize water resistance and facilitate both escape and pursuit. They lead roving, predaceous lives far offshore in deep, clear open ocean, usually hunting near the surface, but also at great depths.

Most fish have temperatures close to that of the surrounding water because they lose body heat through the gills. But tuna can be up to 18 degrees warmer than the sea. They retain body heat by means of a countercurrent heat-exchange system that allows muscle tissue to operate more effectively. As a result, they can swim faster, as well as extend their forays farther north into colder water.

Tuna generally spawn in open ocean. Females lay thousands of millimeter-size eggs, each buoyed by a globule of oil.

Schools of tuna may have over 50,000 individuals. They often feed beneath dolphins. The dolphins attract tuna fishermen who capture the tuna in big, bag-like purse seines. The process also traps, and drowns, the air-breathing dolphins, often significantly reducing their numbers. There has also been a substantial worldwide decline in some tuna species, particularly bluefins. Progress is being made to reduce the number of dolphins killed in tuna fishing, but strong conservation measures and improved fishing techniques are needed to save both tuna and dolphins from extermination.

SKIPJACK, SKIPJACK TUNA
Katsuwonus pelamis

To 102 cm (40 in). Dark, slightly metallic blue above, silver below, with four to six horizontal dark bands. Eats other schooling fish. Both sexes mature at about 40 cm. In tropical water, spawning may occur year-round. Highly migratory, traveling in large schools, inshore to offshore. Found worldwide in nearly all oceans. In the Pacific, from British Columbia to Peru.

PACIFIC MACKEREL, CHUB MACKEREL
Scomber japonicus

To 64 cm (25 in). Dark green to bluish-black above, with many wavy streaks passing just below lateral line. Lower sides silvery with dark blotches. Dorsal fins widely separated. Eats schooling fish (anchovies, herring) and squid. Spawns near shore, April–July, possibly more than once per year, each time producing several hundred thousand pelagic eggs that hatch in three days. Many mature in second year. A highly migratory, schooling fish. Found from surface to 200 fathoms. From Gulf of Alaska to Chile.

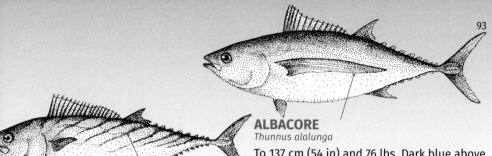

ALBACORE
Thunnus alalunga

To 137 cm (54 in) and 76 lbs. Dark blue above, silvery white below. First dorsal fin deep yellow. Second dorsal and anal fins light yellow. Has extremely long pectoral fin. Eats pilchards, herring, anchovies, sauries, small rockfish, squid, and euphasiid shrimp, near the surface. In turn, it is eaten by striped marlins and other fish. Spawns January–June, southwest of Hawaii. Migrates to mid-Pacific, sometimes Japan, in winter; returns to California coast in summer. Can move 6 miles per day but, aided by upwelling currents off the Oregon coast, may cover 15 miles. Seems to prefer clear offshore water. Usually in large schools. Worldwide. In the Pacific, from southern Alaska to southern Baja California.

PACIFIC BONITO
Sarda chiliensis

To 102 cm (40 in). Greenish-blue above, silver below, with oblique stripes on back. Eats sardines, anchovies, pelagic fish, and squid. Spawns January–May (southern California). Inshore and pelagic, in schools. From Alaska to southern Baja California, but rare north of California. A more southern population is found off the coast of Peru.

94

BLUEFIN TUNA
Thunnus thynnus

To 188 cm (78 in), but some known to reach 304 cm (120 in). Most in Pacific area weigh 10–45 lbs. Largest known weighed over 1,490 lbs. Dark blue to black on back, silver below. Belly has white spots and lines. First dorsal fin is blue and yellow; second dorsal is reddish-brown. Has short pectoral fin. A speedy, voracious predator, the bluefin eats squid and schooling fish (anchovies, jack mackerel, sardines) and is occasionally eaten by sperm whales. Some from Pacific Coast migrate to Japan. Found inshore and offshore, worldwide. On Pacific Coast, from Shelikof Strait to south of Baja California.

YELLOWFIN TUNA
Thunnus albacares

To 193 cm (75.6 in) and 125 lbs in Pacific Coast area. Dark blue above, silvery gray below. Some have yellow side stripe. Fins yellowish. Young have white bars and spots on belly. An aggressive, fast-swimming predator, the yellowfin eats various schooling fishes. Forms large schools. Found offshore, in open ocean, at surface to 138 fathoms. Lives in Atlantic, Pacific, and Indian Oceans. On Pacific Coast, from Point Conception to Chile.

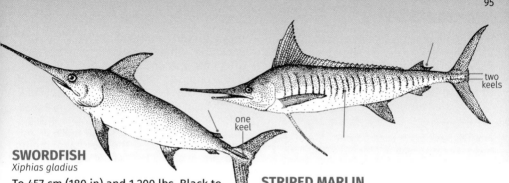

one keel

two keels

SWORDFISH
Xiphias gladius

To 457 cm (180 in) and 1,200 lbs. Black to brownish-black above, light brown below. Adult lacks scales, pelvic fins, and teeth on jaws. A speedy predator that feeds on various fish, squid, and pelagic crustaceans. May use "sword" to stun or kill prey. During whaling era, swords of this fish and billfish were often found broken off in the wooden hulls of ships, sometimes causing leaks. Found inshore and offshore, surface to 300 fathoms. Migratory, usually solitary, and worldwide. On Pacific Coast, from Oregon to Chile.

STRIPED MARLIN
Tetrapturus audax

To 408 cm (160 in). Dark blue above, silvery white below. Sides have 15–25 blue bars or vertical rows of spots. Jaws have teeth. Adult has pelvic fins and scales. Eats fish, squid, pelagic crabs, and shrimp. Spawns May–August in northern Pacific. Found at surface to mid depths, offshore, but common around oceanic islands in Pacific and Indian Oceans. From Cape Mendocino to Chile, but more prevalent south of Point Conception.

FLATFISH BIOLOGY

Halibut, flounder, sole, turbot, sanddabs, and tonguefish are generally known as flatfish. Of 822 flatfish species, most are marine. They range in size from tiny sanddabs 15 cm (6 in) long to Atlantic halibut over 300 cm (10 ft) long and 700 pounds.

Flatfish have both eyes on one side of the head. They lack swim bladders. They rest the eyeless side on the bottom, where their flat form offers minimal resistance to strong currents and allows them to easily maintain position. They often bury themselves in the sand or mud with rhythmic fin movements, leaving only eyes and mouth exposed. Many can change color to match surroundings.

When flatfish spawn, females release their eggs into open water. Eggs of some species have oil droplets that make them float. Other species' eggs lack oil and sink. Eggs may hatch in seven or more days, depending on temperature. At first, flatfish larvae look like most fish, with one eye on each side of the head. Within about 24 days after hatching, one eye begins to migrate to the opposite side of the head. Species in which the left eye moves to the right side of the head are called **right-eyed,** and vice versa. Most species are strictly one or the other. A few species have both right- or left-eyed individuals. The location of mouth and gill cover will help you determine whether they are right or left. Once eye migration is complete, the young fish settle to the bottom blind-side down. Flatfish are extremely important to us as food. Unfortunately, some Pacific halibut have been found with higher-than-acceptable levels of methyl mercury in their flesh.

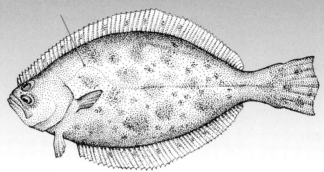

CALIFORNIA HALIBUT
Paralichthys californicus

To 152 cm (60 in). Uniformly dark brown to black, often mottled light/dark. Key features are large mouth, sharp teeth, and lateral line arched over pectoral fin. Usually left-eyed, but some have eyes on right. Eats anchovies, queenfish, and squid. Often feeds off the bottom, but may leap out of water in pursuit of surface schools of anchovies. Eaten by angel sharks, electric rays, sea lions, and dolphins. Spawns in shallow water, February–July. Males mature at 2 to 3 years, females at 4 to 5 years. Found on sandy bottom inshore to 100 fathoms. Tagging studies show that this species does not move far from settling site—some to 140 miles maximum. Common near entrances to many harbors, bays, and estuaries. From northern Washington to southern Baja California.

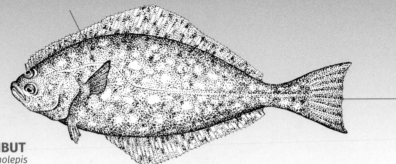

PACIFIC HALIBUT
Hippoglossus stenolepis

To 267 cm (105 in) and 500 lbs, but a few to 800 lbs. Our largest flatfish. Dark brown to blackish, with spots, mottling. Almost always right-eyed. Jaw does not extend past middle of eye, as it does in California halibut. Eats fish, crabs, clams, squid, and other invertebrates. Spawns November–January at 150–225 fathoms. Large females can produce 2–3 million eggs. Larvae are concentrated mainly below 109 fathoms. When halibut is 18 mm long, eye on left side begins migration to right side. As larvae grow, they rise and drift inshore. They settle on bottom when 6 to 7 months old, then move offshore at 5 to 7 years. Found from surface to 600 fathoms, but usually above 225 fathoms. May migrate 1,000 miles. From Bering Sea to northern Channel Islands.

ROCK SOLE *Lepidopsetta bilineata*

To 60 cm (23.5 in). Light to dark brown or gray, sometimes mottled with red or yellow. Lateral line arches abruptly over pectoral fin with a short branch along back that ends before arch. Adults eat clam siphons, brittle stars, shrimp, worms, and small fish. Females lay to 1.3 million eggs, February–April. Found on gravelly bottom, scarce below 200 fathoms, usually at less than 100. Lives in Sea of Japan, and in Pacific from Bering Sea to Tanner Bank.

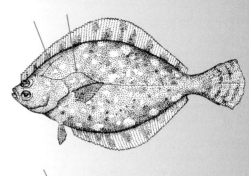

C-O TURBOT, C-O SOLE
Pleuronichthys coenosus

To 36 cm (14 in). Dark brown to blackish with conspicuous dark spot at midbody. Caudal fin has dark spot preceded by backwards C-shaped bar. Long branch of lateral line along back reaches midbody. Four to six dorsal rays extend over to blind side. Young are found inshore, adults offshore to 190 fathoms, over sandy and rocky bottoms. From southern Alaska to northern Baja California.

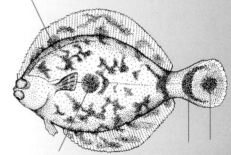

SPOTTED TURBOT
Pleuronichthys ritteri

To 29 cm (11.5 in). Brown to grayish-brown, with small light spots. One, or sometimes two or three, dark spot at back of dorsal fin and at midbody. First six rays of dorsal fin on blind side. Found inshore, to 25 fathoms. From Morro Bay to southern Baja California.

CURLFIN TURBOT, CURLFIN SOLE
Pleuronichthys decurrens

To 37 cm (14.5 in). Mottled brown, blackish, reddish-brown. Branch of lateral line passes along back past midbody. Right-eyed. First 9–12 dorsal rays are on blind side. Eggs are pelagic and hatch after seven days. Found on sandy or muddy bottom to 290 fathoms. From Prince William Sound to north-central Baja California.

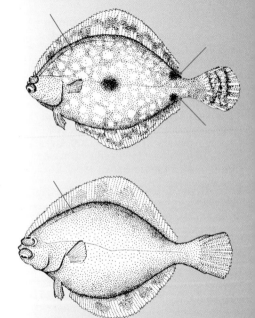

DIAMOND TURBOT *Hypsopsetta guttulata*

To 46 cm (18 in). Dark gray to greenish, often with bright blue-gray spots. Yellow on underside of mouth. lateral-line branch along back more than halfway to caudal fin. Right-eyed. Found on muddy or sandy bottom to 25 fathoms. From Cape Mendocino to Magdalena Bay.

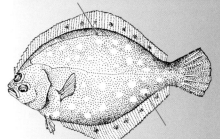

ENGLISH SOLE, LEMON SOLE
Parophrys vetulus

To 57 cm (22.5 in). Brown, occasionally spotted. Belly side white, pale yellow, tinted red. Upper eye visible from blind side. Eats clams, clam siphons, worms, shrimp, small crabs, and brittle stars. Spawns January–March (British Columbia). Eggs pelagic, but sink several hours before hatching. Hatch in 90-plus hours, depending on temperature. Young are about 20 cm long at 2 years. Young are found in shallow water, but adults shift between shallows in spring and deeper water in winter. To 300 fathoms. Highly migratory, ranging 700 miles or more. From Unimak Island to Baja California.

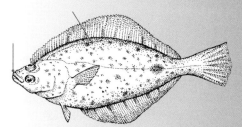

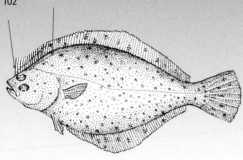

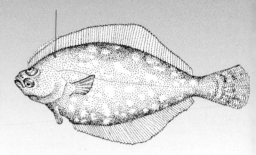

SAND SOLE
Psettichthys melanostichus

To 63 cm (25 in). Gray, brown, or greenish with black speckles. Lateral line has low arch over pectoral, with short branch along back. First five to eight dorsal rays mostly free of membrane. Right-eyed. Eats speckled sanddabs, herring, anchovies, crabs, shrimp, and worms. Spawns January–July. Eggs hatch in about five days. Mostly found in shallow, inshore waters, but some to 100 fathoms or deeper. From Bering Sea to Redondo Beach, southern California.

BUTTER SOLE
Isopsetta isolepis

To 55 cm (22 in) but usually less than 30 cm. Brown with dark and light mottling; sometimes lightly spotted in yellow or green. Yellow on edges of dorsal and anal fins. Lateral line has low arch over pectoral fin. Right-eyed. Eats worms, shrimp, sand dollars, and young herring. Spawns February–April. Lives 10–11 years (34–39 cm). Migrates to shallow water in summer, deep water in winter. Found to 200 fathoms but usually at lesser depth. From Bering Sea to Ventura.

REX SOLE
Glyptocephalus zachirus

To 59 cm (23 in). Light brown; fins dark-edged with long pectoral fin mostly black. Lateral line straight, unbranched. Small mouth. Right-eyed. Biology not well-known. Spawns in spring. Slow-growing. Lives to 24 years. Found offshore to 350 fathoms, most abundant below 33 fathoms. From Bering Sea to northern Baja California.

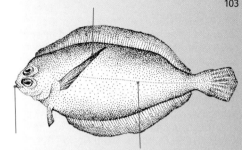

DOVER SOLE
Microstomus pacificus

To 76 cm (30 in). Brown; fins dusky. Blind side light to dark gray, sometimes with red areas. Slimy and slippery. Right-eyed. Eats burrowing animals like worms, shrimp, and clams (siphons). Spawns November–February (California). Eggs pelagic. Unlike other flatfish, eye migration and physical transformation is delayed for months. Females grow faster and live longer. North–south migration of 100–350 miles occurs. Found over mud bottom to 600 fathoms. From Bering Sea to central Baja California.

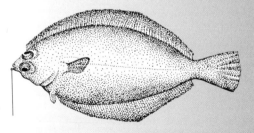

PETRALE SOLE *Eopsetta jordani*

To 70 cm (27 in). Brown. Dorsal and anal fins have faint blotches. Right-eyed. Large mouth. Eats shrimp, sand lance, herring, and various other bottom animals. Spawning occurs at 200 fathoms, in late winter or early spring (British Columbia). Female lives up to 25 years, male up to 19. Moves into deep water in winter, but spends rest of year in shallow water. To 250 fathoms. From Bering Sea to northern Baja California.

STARRY FLOUNDER *Platichthys stellatus*

To 91 cm (36 in). Brown to nearly black. Dorsal, anal, caudal fins have dark bars alternating with yellow-orange bars. Rough tubercles (modified scales) on body. Can be right- or left-eyed. Eats crabs, shrimp, worms, clams, and small fish. Spawns in shallows, December–January (California, later in north). Found inshore in bays, estuaries, outer coast, to 150 fathoms or more. Japan; from Bering Sea to Santa Barbara.

PACIFIC SANDDAB
Citharichthys sordidus

To 41 cm (16 in). Light brown mottled with dark brown, sometimes with yellow-orange spots. Bony ridge above lower eye. Left-eyed. Eats worms, small crustaceans, and young anchovies. Spawns from February (Puget Sound) to September (California). Some females may spawn twice. Half of females are mature at 19 cm long. Lives to 12 years. Found on soft bottom to 300 fathoms. From Bering Sea to southern Baja California.

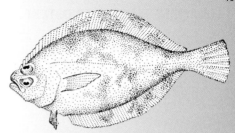

SPECKLED SANDDAB
Citharichtbys stigmaeus

To 17 cm (7 in), but rarely over 13 cm. Brown to tan with speckles, spots. Ridge above lower eye absent. Left-eyed. Eats small crustaceans and worms. In turn, it is eaten by sea birds, sea lions, seals, and other fish. Spawns March–September. Found in inshore, shallow waters (50 fathoms), sometimes to 200 fathoms, on sand or mud bottom. Common in bays and estuaries. From southern Alaska to southern Baja California.

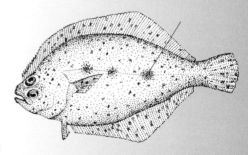

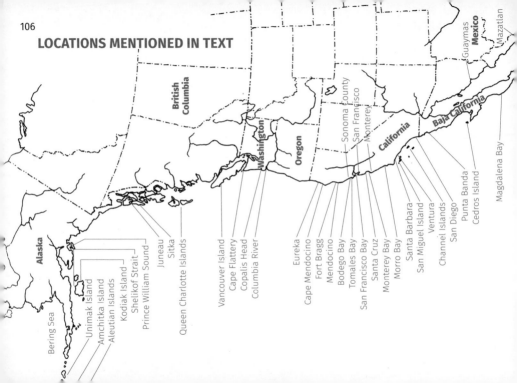

106

LOCATIONS MENTIONED IN TEXT

British Columbia

Alaska

Mexico

Guaymas

Mazatlan

Baja California

California

Oregon

Washington

Sonoma County

San Francisco

Monterey

Bering Sea

Unimak Island

Amchitka Island

Aleutian Islands

Kodiak Island

Shelikof Strait

Prince William Sound

Juneau

Sitka

Queen Charlotte Islands

Vancouver Island

Cape Flattery

Copalis Head

Columbia River

Eureka

Cape Mendocino

Fort Bragg

Mendocino

Bodega Bay

Tomales Bay

San Francisco Bay

Santa Cruz

Monterey Bay

Morro Bay

Santa Barbara

San Miguel Island

Ventura

Channel Islands

San Diego

Punta Banda

Cedros Island

Magdalena Bay

INDEX

Other books in the pocket-size *Finder* series:

NATURE STUDY GUIDES are published by AdventureKEEN, 2204 1st Ave. S., Suite 102, Birmingham, AL 35233; 800-678-7006; naturestudy.com. See shop.adventurewithkeen.com for our full line of nature and outdoor activity guides by ADVENTURE PUBLICATIONS, MENASHA RIDGE PRESS, and WILDERNESS PRESS, including many guides for birding, wildflowers, rocks, and trees, plus regional and national parks, hiking, camping, backpacking, and more.